Healthy Scorecard

Delivering Breakthrough Results that Employees and Investors will Love!

Danielle Pratt, BSR, MBA

© 2001 Danielle Pratt. All rights reserved.

No part of this publication may be reproduced, stored in a retrieval system, or transmitted, in any form or by any means, electronic, mechanical, photocopying, recording, or otherwise, without the prior written permission of the author.

Printed in Canada

Layout/typesetting:
VRG design & publishing services
www.inetex.com/vivencia

```
Canadian Cataloguing in Publication Data
Pratt, Danielle, 1961-
   The healthy scorecard

      Includes bibliographical references and index.
      ISBN 1-55212-557-2

      1. Strategic planning.  2. Organizational
   effectiveness--Evaluation.  3. Industrial productivity--
   Measurement.
   I. Title.
   HD30.28.P73 2001          658.4'012            C00-911439-4
```

TRAFFORD

This book was published *on-demand* in cooperation with Trafford Publishing.
On-demand publishing is a unique process and service of making a book available for retail sale to the public taking advantage of on-demand manufacturing and Internet marketing. **On-demand publishing** includes promotions, retail sales, manufacturing, order fulfilment, accounting and collecting royalties on behalf of the author.

Suite 6E, 2333 Government St., Victoria, B.C. V8T 4P4, CANADA
Phone   250-383-6864   Toll-free   1-888-232-4444 (Canada & US)
Fax   250-383-6804   E-mail   sales@trafford.com
Web site   www.trafford.com   TRAFFORD PUBLISHING IS A DIVISION OF TRAFFORD HOLDINGS LTD.
Trafford Catalogue #00-0223   www.trafford.com/robots/00-0223.html

10   9   8   7   6   5   4   3   2   1

To Mister and The VP's
My life partners and spiritual bank

TESTIMONIALS

The Healthy Scorecard *makes the business case for linking employee health to organizational performance irresistible. This is a "breakthrough" book for executives seeking untapped sources of competitive advantage—in the improved health and productivity of their own employees.*

A bravura intellectual and artistic performance!

Sean Sullivan
President and CEO,
Institute for Health and Productivity Management

"A passionately written and extremely well researched book. ***The Healthy Scorecard*** *makes a strong and compelling case for the links between health, leadership, and business results."*

Jim Clemmer
President of The CLEMMER Group
and best-selling author, Firing on All Cylinders,
and Pathways to Performance

"Compelling! Pratt has clearly raised the bar on measurement as an integral part of organization performance. As she points out in the book, it is the entire cycle of measurement that really counts. Don't just measure.... but measure the right things, do it frequently, understand the correlation, and take action for needed change."

Owen Griffiths
Senior Consultant
Tecskor Software Inc.

In a word, EXCELLENT!... the book delivers a real punch on the results side which it needs to do to be credible for executives.

The research is deep, intense, and hard to ignore... The case study examples from clients and other leading organizations are solid validation of the case presented. The links to the state-of-art management practices (Strategy Map, Service Profit Chain, Gallup 12) are further validation of the business case.

I especially like the message that simple, functional, and standard measurement can work (one size does indeed fit all in this particular area of performance measurement for Employee Capability/Wellbeing). Danielle Pratt is absolutely right here and it is a refreshing challenge to those who inanely pursue measurement purity with an unnecessary level of scientific precision. It is after all not nearly as complicated as we want to make it.

An outstanding piece of work!

Mark Henderson
Executive Vice President,
The Clemmer Group

"Danielle Pratt has created new food for thought and in doing so is making a major contribution to the recipes for business success in the new millennium. I have long tried to convince leaders that focusing on the people in our organizations is the essential key to being world leaders. Finally, with this work building on the work of so many leading thinkers in quality, leadership, and health, she has created the most compelling business argument to date. The health of an organization is the most important indicator of success because it permeates every system in the organization- in fact, it is the stuff that binds. This book makes us look at the very nature of the system of quality, health, and safety as it is currently practiced.

This is scary stuff, and a must-read for executives interested in high performance."

Maureen Shaw, President and CEO
Industrial Accident Prevention Association,
one of *Canada's Top 100 Employers*

"Our worklife transcends every aspect of our lives. This book begins a critical investigation into being engaged in your work and the actual health of not only the individual employee, but also the family. Organizations everywhere are beginning to understand the link between having the right person in the right job, and the overall impact this has upon the health of people and the organization. The **Healthy Scorecard** demonstrates that what's good for employees and what's good for companies are not separate poles anymore!"

Curt W. Coffman
Global Practice Leader
The Gallup Organization
Co-Author, *First, Break all the Rules*

CONTENTS

How to Skim this Book xvii
Preface xix

SECTION I
THE HEALTH/HIGH PERFORMANCE SYNERGY

1. The Untapped Frontier 3
  Good Health is Good Leadership is Great Business...
  and we can prove it! 4
  Employee Wellbeing:
  New Weapon in the War for Talent 4
  Accounting for "Health Capital" 6
  Opportunity Costs: The Underside of the
  Health Cost Iceberg 7

2. Redefining Health and the
  Balanced Scorecard 11
  What is the Balanced Scorecard? 12
  What's Wrong with the Balanced Scorecard? 14
  Massaging the Balanced Scorecard 14
  Debunking Health Myths 20
  The New Frontier for High Performance 26
  Leadership Check-Up 28

3. Top Box Results 31
Raising the Bar on Performance:
Top Box Results 31
"Top Box" Customer Results 41
"Top Box" Employee Results 44
Toward Stakeholder Balance 47
Sustainable High Performance 51
Leadership Check-Up 59

4. Good Health is Good Leadership 61
Looking for Health in all the Wrong Places 61
A New Paradigm for Health 65
Research Highlights: The Healthiest Companies 65
Research Highlights: Employee Capability,
Engagement, and Commitment 86
Connecting the Dots 95
Leadership Check-Up 97

5. If Quality can be Free,
Health can be Too! 99
Footprints From the Quality Journey 99
Accounting for the Cost of Quality 100
Accounting for the Cost of Health 101
The Cost of Opting Out 116
Leadership Check-Up 121

SECTION II
THE HEALTHY SCORECARD

6. Linking Health into The Balanced Scorecard 125
   Untapped Excellence: The Sears Model 125
   Other Untapped Health Indices 131
   The Employee Capability/Wellbeing Index© 137
   A Closer Look at the Healthy Corporate Scorecard 157
   Color-Coding Your Measurement Strategy 167
   Building Alignment 173
   Building Nimbleness 174
   How Quickly can we turn around Organizational Health? 176
   What about Small Businesses? 177
   Human Resources, and Health and Safety Scorecards .. 178
   Leadership Check-Up 181

7. The Big Picture 183
   The Lever for Change: Institutional Investors 183
   Get Rich Quick! 186
   Cultivating Demanding Stakeholders 188
   The 5th Perspective: Societal 190
   The Future: Intersecting Balanced Scorecards 196
   Closing 198
   Leadership Check-Up 203

FURTHER READING
Acknowledgements 207
Putting More Health Myths to Rest 215
Notes 231

How to Skim this Book

I want you to skim this book. After all, that's what I do when I'm deciding where to invest my time. Let's assume that you're facing the same *time famine* as many of my colleagues, and jump right to the highlights.

I'm here not only to help you generate dissatisfaction with the current state, but also to show you what vast improvements the Healthy Scorecard offers. *Bon appétit!*

<u>*Key points to skim*</u>

Here is the learning that you won't want to miss:

▶ *What drives superior and sustained business results?* Take a look at the Sears 10-point index and the Gallup 12 on pages 127, 130, and 133.

▶ *New thinking - What really makes workplaces healthy?* A summary of the research is presented in Chapter 4, page 85.

▶ *Good health is good leadership is great business... and we can prove it!* The *pièce de résistance* – the Healthy Strategy Map©, and Healthy Profit Chain, presented on pages 143 and 145.

▶ *Easy money* - How investors will profit from this synergy – and drive demand for healthier workplaces, on pages 186-188.

▶ *Leadership Check-ups* – Self-assessments at the end of each Chapter.

Skim these... and then come back for more!

PREFACE

I was chomping at the bit to write this book three years ago. What a blessing that it got delayed! Organizational health was an exciting field in the 90's, but now, thanks to the Balanced Scorecard, Service Profit Chain, and War for Talent, it's irresistible… and not only to the choir, but also to executives and investors.

In writing *The Healthy Scorecard*, I have merely woven threads between existing research on the leadership/health connection, and recent practice in predicting employee-customer-financial linkages. But as you'll see in this book, the two fields are like one. The biggest surprise is that this synergy is untapped.

So this is not a technical book about employee health and safety. It's a practical management book about *sustainable* high performance. The problem is, any leader serious about leveraging human capital must understand what makes employees tick—and what ticks them off. And it turns out that if we understand the common drivers of human motivation, we also capture the drivers of stress, illness, and injury.

Why is this a Must-Read for Executives?

Why is *The Healthy Scorecard* a must-read? Because it opens the door to a phenomenal, untapped improvement potential in sustainable high performance: the synergy between great leaders, *healthy and capable employees,* satisfied and loyal customers, and yes—the bottom line.

I would bet that you aren't making the link between employee health and business strategy yet. But you will.

The Seeds for this Book

This book would have neither strategic nor clinical "umph" without the groundbreaking work of the following thought leaders:

- *The fathers of the Balanced Scorecard:* Dr. Robert S. Kaplan and Dr. David P. Norton;
- *The chroniclers of the Service Profit Chain:* Professors James L. Heskett, W. Earl Sasser, and Leonard A. Schlesinger;
- *The trailblazers in jaw-dropping predictive Employee-Customer-Profit Chains:* Dr. Steve Kirn, Vice President of Innovation and Organization Development, and his leadership team at Sears Roebuck and Co.;
- *The economic historians and sustainable value sleuths:* James C. Collins and Jerry I. Porras, acclaimed authors of *Built to Last;*
- *The pioneers in the "Good health is good leadership" research:* Robert Karasek and Töres Theorell; and
- *Canadian health researchers extraordinaire:* Dr. Martin Shain and Dr. Terrence Sullivan.

Thanks to the work of these luminaries, my personal learning curve has just rocketed. And with it, my ability to articulate this exhilarating and untapped new frontier in high performance. I like to think of myself as the *remora* – the intrepid fish with a suction cup on the top of its head – that attaches itself underneath the jaw of the shark, and catches the morsels which the shark doesn't eat. I'm just hanging on for the ride – and keeping the host healthy in the process.

I would like to thank the following organizations for their financial support in producing this book: *Health Canada's Population Health Fund*; Canada's *Centre for Addiction and Mental Health*; and *Glaxo Wellcome Inc*. All three organizations share a vision to make employee health a vital part of business strategy, and together, we are making exciting inroads!

I am also deeply indebted to a tenacious group of allies who have stood by me in the writing of this book. Most notably, my husband Tim, the epitome of what a life partner can be. And Ken Boutilier, an early adopter with a vision - and pit bull tendencies - who simply didn't let go of this project. My professional acknowledgements can be found – in their profusion! - throughout this book, as well as in the Further Reading chapter. I extend my profound thanks to all of my supporters who made this vision a reality.

Danielle Pratt, BSR, MBA
President, Healthy Business Inc.
Calgary, Alberta
January, 2001

Section I

THE HEALTH/HIGH PERFORMANCE SYNERGY

*Good health
is good leadership
is great business*

1

THE UNTAPPED FRONTIER

When Sears Roebuck proved that they earned $200 million extra in 1997 as a result of improving employee satisfaction by 4%, they paved the way for us to capture the true costs of poor wellbeing.[1]

For the past decade I've been kicking tires, looking for the business case to make employee wellbeing *irresistible* to managers. Like many people, I've intuitively felt that preventing stress, illness, and injury makes great business sense.

But intuition isn't enough. We need numbers that go beyond trivial cost savings. We need numbers to prove that employee wellbeing is a key *driver* of enduring corporate performance and yes—profits.

Unfortunately, the Holy Grail of opportunity costs—the dollar tag for lost productivity, innovation and resilience—had eluded me. It wasn't until I stumbled across the predictive linkages of the Employee-Customer-Profit Chain that I had the karmic "Aha!". *This* is what I've been looking for all these years.

Good Health is Good Leadership is Great Business... *and we can prove it!*

Thanks to the Balanced Scorecard and Service Profit Chain, we can now capture the huge underbelly of the health cost iceberg: the opportunity costs of lost productivity, innovation, and resilience. We can finally measure exactly how much these losses affect the bottom line.

And these costs are monstrous.

The early adopters of quality recoiled when they realized just how much poor quality was costing them. We're at the same point for wellbeing—most organizations have no clue how badly they're hemorrhaging.

Employee Wellbeing: New Weapon in the War for Talent

We have a new weapon in the War for Talent. At the cutting edge of practice, winning organizations in the private and public sector are developing cause-and-effect Healthy Scorecards which predict the impact of leadership on employee wellbeing and capability, customer results, and the bottom line. These organizations stand to realize huge incremental gains thanks to their strategic focus on health. And in doing so, these organizations are entering a new frontier, a quantum leap in financial performance.

This book will teach you how to make that quantum leap:

- ➤ ***Learn*** what makes executives and investors lean forward in their seats when they hear about this new improvement opportunity.
- ➤ ***Find out*** why employee wellbeing is the latest untapped frontier in the War for Talent.
- ➤ ***Get the numbers*** on why a Strategic Health Focus pays. And,
- ➤ ***Build*** a Balanced Scorecard that unleashes the huge untapped potential of Employee Health.

Employee wellbeing is one area where leaders can truly have their cake and eat it too. For it turns out that the drivers of employee capability—the ability to deliver results to customers—almost exactly mirror the key drivers of employee wellbeing. In short, we can lead for health and high performance, and this is what makes success endure.

It's time to call a spade a spade.
Good health is good leadership is great business... and now, thanks to the Predictive Balanced Scorecard, we can prove it!

Accounting for "Health Capital"

> *"If you can't measure what you want,
> then you start wanting what you can measure."*
>
> Robert Kaplan
> BSC for Government Conference 2000[2]

We are entering a New Age in accounting. As Dr. Kaplan, co-author of *The Balanced Scorecard* rightly proposes, it is time for us to break new ground with our strategic measurement systems, to measure what we *need*—and not to perseverate with the measures that we have. And this requires us to enter the murky measurement frontier of the intangibles.

Traditionalists may well recoil at the soft measures… the voodoo economics of *"Health Capital"*. But the numbers are on our side.

Account for trailing indicators such as profits, return on equity, lost time injuries, health costs, and you know where you've been. Account for leading indicators such as leadership bench strength, internal service/quality, and employee attitudes, and you'll not only get a peek at where you're going, you can improve your course along the way.

We've been messing up so royally with our myopic accounting practices that organizations are hemorrhaging due to *preventable* stress, illness, and injury. Most know it hurts, but they don't know why.

If the New Economy is surfing on brainpower, we must understand what creates the wave—and how to ride it. This requires that we develop a Strategic Health Focus, and understand the determinants of employee health, capability, and motivation.

OPPORTUNITY COSTS: THE UNDERSIDE OF THE HEALTH COST ICEBERG

But for us to adopt a Strategic Health Focus, leaders need to be convinced that health pays. True, there will always be stellar organizations and leaders for whom this is a no-brainer, and who invest in health on humanitarian grounds. But even this is a risky proposition.

What happens when the supportive CEO leaves?

For health to be widely embraced in the business community as a strategic business imperative, we need to step up to the plate with some numbers. And I've been finding numbers that **excite** executives and investors!

Traditionally, we have captured *direct costs* such as Worker's Compensation, short and long-term disability costs, and drug costs. These are substantial in their own right. B.C. Hydro for example incurred over $20 Million in direct health costs in 1999. As Ken Webb, Manager of Corporate Health and Safety noted,

> *"We'd really be paying attention to $20 million of maintenance costs in one of our generators. We'd really be paying attention to $20 million of maintenance in one of our transmission lines.*

> *Perhaps we ought to be starting to pay a little more attention to $20 million in maintenance for our human capital."*
>
> Ken Webb
> *The Development of a Health Report*[3]

We have also measured ***indirect costs*** such as the cost of equipment damage or replacement labour as part of our business case. Admittedly, I've been absorbed by the tales of clients or my audiences, such as the City of Calgary, which incurs a tab for indirect costs of $300,000 if a garbage truck gets trashed in an accident[4], or the Department of National Defence, which suffers a $30 Million dollar tab for equipment replacement, if a fighter jet crashes.[5]

But it wasn't until I stumbled across Rucci's *"Employee-Customer-Profit Chain at Sears"* article in *Harvard Business Review*[6]—and then the latest work on predictive Balanced Scorecards by Robert Kaplan and the Balanced Scorecard Collaborative, that I had the big "WOW"!

Until recently we have merely been tinkering with "Good" and "Bad" employee health costs. Now we can get down to business with the mother lode of health costs: the "Ugly" costs of eroded employee wellbeing… the opportunity costs of lost productivity, innovation, and resilience.

Since my baptism with the Service Profit Chain and Balanced Scorecard, I have finally been able to put numbers to the opportunity costs of health. And as my RBI[7] has gone up, so have the requests increased for me to write this book.

The message of the '90's was, "You should do this… it's the right thing to do."

Framed by the Balanced Scorecard and War for Talent, the message of the new millennium for employee wellbeing is, "You can't afford NOT to do this!"

2

REDEFINING HEALTH AND THE BALANCED SCORECARD

"Following the light of the sun, we left the Old World."

Inscription on Columbus' caravels

We begin this journey by debunking a few of my favorite myths. These all have a healthy dose of controversy, and will hopefully play havoc on dearly-held beliefs about health. Most of all, I hope to stimulate some much-needed debate on the value of organizational health, and its potent contribution to superior business results.

And while I am an enthusiastic devotée of the Balanced Scorecard (BSC), I'm also going to address what I see as an important opportunity to push the envelope.

The targeted myths fall into two categories:

- *Balanced Scorecard;* and
- *Health*

But lest you are not familiar with the Balanced Scorecard, let's first level the playing field.

WHAT IS THE BALANCED SCORECARD?

The Balanced Scorecard, created by Harvard Business School professor Dr. Robert Kaplan, and Balanced Scorecard Collaborative President, Dr. David Norton, is hailed as one of the greatest management advances in the 20th Century.[8] It focuses leadership attention on the critical drivers of future performance, thereby enabling organizations to anticipate—and change—their future. And it provides a line of sight to link individual employees with the strategy.

Traditional accounting systems focus on results that have already happened, such as financial performance, or injury rates. Much like driving while looking in a rear-view mirror, this approach is informative in a retrospective, dangerous kind of way. The Balanced Scorecard, on the other hand, captures both leading and trailing indicators: the past, and the future. Most important, it is designed to show *cause-and-effect* in an organization's strategy. The BSC is a living, evolving, learning tool for the whole organization, which tells the story of the organization's strategy. It tells leaders – typically in 20-25 key measures—what works, and why.

In building a BSC, a leadership team identifies a vision and strategy for the organization, and then crafts key objectives, measures, and targets for each of the "Perspectives": Financial, Customer, Process, and Learning and Growth. Key objectives are cascaded down to business units, ensuring powerful alignment to the organization's strategy. Resources are channeled to initiatives which are aligned with the strategic objectives. In other words, everyone is singing from the same song sheet.

BSC's are meant to be crafted from the top-down. That is, the executive team sequentially addresses the questions:

1) *What are our **Vision**, **Mission**, and **Strategy**?*
2) *Given our Strategy what are the key **Financial results** we need to achieve?*
3) *To achieve these Financial results, which **Customer results** do we need to deliver?*
4) *To achieve these Customer results, which key **Internal Business Processes** do we need to excel at?; and finally,*
5) *To excel at our key Internal Business Processes, which **Learning and Growth outcomes** do we need to achieve?*

The power of the Balanced Scorecard is that it focuses leadership attention and resources on the critical drivers of the business—the measures which are key to the successful execution of strategy.

The Balanced Scorecard demands answers to the questions, "What will we do?", as well as, "What will we NOT do?".

And in doing so, the BSC siphons resources away from non-strategic initiatives.

What's Wrong with the Balanced Scorecard?

And herein lies the danger. Because if your Balanced Scorecard is constructed top-down, and your Internal Process objectives are too narrowly focused, you may entirely miss the mark with your Learning and Growth measures.

And even if your market strategy and strategic execution are spectacular, you may miss the boat on the basic human capital drivers.

And this leads us to Myths #1 and #2.

Massaging the Balanced Scorecard

Myth #1: If you have a BSC, you've captured the Human Performance Engine.

> "The best way to build strategy maps
> is from the top down."
>
> Kaplan R.S., Norton D.P.,
> *Harvard Business Review*[9]

The Balanced Scorecard is hailed as one of the most significant management advances of the 20th Century.[10] But it has an Achilles Heel.

Fact:

I submit that there is a significant flaw in the way many BSC's are crafted. And this flaw leads to complacency that human performance issues have been successfully dealt with. This flaw arises from the traditional top-down construction of BSC objectives, which tends to provide a customer-centric view of success.

Leaders are encouraged to identify their vision and strategy, to pinpoint the financial and customer results they need to achieve to fulfill their vision… and then to identify the Internal Processes they need to excel at, in order to deliver said Financial and Customer results. Learning and Growth objectives tend to be crafted so they will maximize success in the chosen Internal Process and Customer objectives.

But what if the chosen Internal Processes are too narrowly focused? Or if the core strategy—on which BSC objectives are based—is flawed, and under-represents the human performance engine? Fact is, this domino effect can be dangerous. And it has the greatest impact on the Learning and Growth perspective.

Further, if your health and human resources initiatives are not *explicitly* linked with corporate BSC objectives, you run the very real risk that core human capital initiatives will be slashed.

When it comes to Human Capital, the Balanced Scorecard's greatest strength— and weakness—is strategic focus!

In my view, we need to build BSC's from the bottom-up, *as well as* from the top-down. In fact, I am convinced that there are some common motivators of human performance—and wellbeing—which should be captured in *every* corporate scorecard.

So while the intent of a Strategy Map is to identify the destination first, and then the path to get there[11], the BSC does need to be rooted on firm ground. That is, we need to craft Learning and Growth measures which also capture the essential motivators of human performance.

On the one hand, this is easy to do. Because if we are to remain true to the intent of the BSC—which is brevity and clarity—we should be targeting a *limited* number of employee measures. And by necessity, this steers us to the very basic motivators of human performance. In fact, when you get to a list this short, I believe these motivators transcend culture and workplace type. (More on this in Chapter 6).

But the harsh reality is that many leaders don't know precisely what these common motivators are. So by default, many Learning and Growth measures—and in turn many BSC's—are weak or incomplete.

> *In building a Balanced Scorecard, we must not only capture the people issues which drive strategy,* **but also** *the common motivators which drive people.*

This isn't to say that strategic measures for Innovation and Growth are not vital. But I'd submit that we need fundamental, as well as strategic measures of human capital.

Yet the prevailing approach is top-down BSC construction. As Dr. Kaplan noted in a recent exchange,

> *"I make the distinction between organizational vital signs: those that are critical to measure, monitor, and act upon to correct when they fall outside specified control limits—but are not the drivers of strategy—versus strategic (BSC) variables: those for which improvement and becoming best-in-class will truly drive performance breakthroughs."*
>
> Dr. Robert Kaplan[12]

This presents a paradox, for while human motivators do not drive strategy *per se*, they most certainly potentiate and sustain it. Perhaps Dr. Kaplan and I are on the same page after all. For I submit that innovative behavior and sustained ability for performance breakthroughs—regardless of the strategy employed—depend on employee capability, motivation, and in turn, wellbeing. And as you'll see from empirical evidence in Chapter 4, when organizations excel at these "generic" soft factors, they make the quantum leap from average performance to sustained high performance. In other words, if you're truly interested in superior business results, satisfactory employee wellbeing just doesn't cut it.

Let me hit this message home with an analogy: Imagine you are an inner-city school teacher, and you've just received the glossy new curriculum for how to teach kids to read. The contents are spectacular—and you just know that these amazing new literacy methods should help. Only problem is, half of the kids in your class come to school without being properly fed or rested. Their sleep is punctuated by gunshot noises, and their homework interrupted by drug-deals. No matter how good your shiny new strategic teaching methods are, if your kids don't have the basics, their learning will suffer.

lesson applies to organizational success. For strat-
[...]y enduring success, we need to feed employees'
[...] and spirits, not just their strategic toolboxes.[13] And this brings us to the psychological and social drivers of health.

The reality is that the Balanced Scorecard can tempt managers to focus on strategic HR measures, and miss out on the basic ones.

Myth #2: All BSC's are Predictive

> *"All animals are equal,
> but some are more equal than others."*
>
> George Orwell
> *Animal Farm*

Many of my clients have challenged my use of the term, "*Predictive* Balanced Scorecard", suggesting that my terminology is redundant. After all, isn't the Balanced Scorecard—by definition—predictive?

In truth, all BSC's are based on the premise that improvements in the soft side of the organization will spill over to hard, financial results. So enhanced results in the Learning and Growth and Internal Processes Perspectives are said to spill over to Customer, and then Financial results. This karmic flow from leading indicators to trailing indicators is indeed the basis of the BSC.

Fact:

Most Balanced Scorecards are only loosely predictive, merely suggesting that as you generally get better in your Learning and Growth, and Internal Business Process areas, your

Customer, and then Financial results will tend to improve. But some BSC's are spectacularly robust, and prove the *causal* linkages between "soft" results, such as employee attitudes, and the bottom line.[14]

*A few organizations have taken the BSC to the next level—where measures in the first two perspectives are used to **predict** customer and financial outcomes with stunning confidence and accuracy.*

It is this next level of predictive power which has so captivated me. In the BSC, we have a means to prove what leaders in the health management field have known for some time: "*Good health is good leadership is great business!*"

But virtually no one uses the predictive BSC for this purpose! Even Sears Roebuck, which has the most sophisticated predictive scorecard in the world[15], has not yet explicitly connected their Employee-Customer-Profit Chain[16] with employee health results. Even Skandia, trailblazer in Intellectual Capital[17] measurement, does not yet *explicitly* map health as a key driver of their outcomes in the Skandia Navigator![18]

Yet health costs are one of the major factors threatening to erode—and eclipse—corporate profits.

The predictive BSC enables us to bridge the awareness gap which until now has misled senior executives to delegate health away from the executive domain. It provides empirical proof that employee health is not only a leadership issue, but also a corporate performance imperative.

DEBUNKING HEALTH MYTHS

Myth #3: Health is a Cost

Take a peek at a typical statement of revenues and expenses, and you'll see health costs reflected as line items, such as extended health costs, drug costs, disability costs, or Worker's Compensation premiums.

The myth that Health is a Cost is fuelled by linear thinking reflected in our traditional silo accounting practices.

So it comes as no surprise that when executives see benefit costs go up, their knee-jerk reaction is panic, then cost-containment. This fight-or-flight reaction will only intensify as our workforce ages, our governments shy away from their role in health, and our ability to more effectively treat and cure disease and disability improves.

One mind-boggling example is that of the Human Genome Project, which just celebrated the decoding of 3.1 billion letters in human DNA on June 26, 2000. As President Clinton commented,

> "With this profound new language,
> humankind is on the verge
> of gaining immense, new power to heal."[19]

In other words, we can expect rocketing up-front health costs, such as drug costs—at least in the short term. But we can also expect dramatic improvements in our ability to reduce pain, suffering, and yes, absenteeism and lost productivity. In fact, there is substantial evidence that if we abdicate our corporate role in employee health, business performance will suffer greatly.

For example, the Human Genome Project will equip us to target medical therapies more effectively. By treating the genotype, physicians will know in advance whether a patient will react negatively to a given medication—saving huge amounts of wasted resources from poorly targeted medications. [20]

> *"Besides speeding up the process and bringing down the cost of drug discovery and development, the new pharmaceutical technology promises three things: **first**, an increase in the range of diseases that are treatable with drugs; **second**, an increase in the precision and effectiveness of those drugs; and **third**, an increase in the ability to anticipate disease, rather than just react to it."*
>
> Geoffrey Carr
> The Economist[21]

Trend lines for health costs over the past decade invoke fear and loathing in many benefits managers. But these trends only capture part of the story, and beg the question, *"Are rising prevention costs a bad thing?"* Shouldn't we expect this as a result of the aging of the workforce? Is a 20% increase in benefits a blessing, considering that demographics should have driven our costs up by 28% this year? Is a 15% increase in drug costs a good thing, considering that we thereby reduced failure costs for absenteeism by 20%?

What value do we get from health benefits? And how does our investment in health add value, or reduce overall costs?

What's missing is Big-Picture accounting that takes into account demographic drivers, the capability of improved therapies to reduce "Failure" costs, and most importantly Total Health Costs.

Fact:

In the absence of an understanding of Total Health Costs, we will ever squeeze one side of the balloon, and avert our eyes when the other side bulges. Or worse yet, not realize that the other side is bulging.

Part of the problem is that the vast majority of organizations do not adequately capture the *indirect* costs of having a stressed, ill, or injured workforce, much less the *opportunity* costs.

Our current accounting practices fly in the face of the systems thinking which revolutionized the quality field. Figure 1 contrasts our traditional approach to quality with the improvements of the past two decades. Quality mavericks such as Philip Crosby won over legions of delighted managers with the notion that "*Quality is Free*".[22] We now know, for example, that our focus for quality improvement needs to be on Total Quality Costs, and that judicious investment in Prevention activities yields returns in the form of lower Failure costs.

We also know that the winners in the Quality movement have translated quality from a cost centre to a profit centre! It would have been beyond our wildest dreams in the '70's that organizations could profitably pursue Six Sigma process quality. But they do.

Figure 1

Where does your Approach to Health fit in?

Quality Then	Quality Now
➤ Root causes poorly understood ➤ Defects relegated to the end of the line ➤ Total Cost impact not recognized ➤ Magnitude of improvement potential not recognized ➤ Knee-jerk reaction to investment	➤ Quality is everyone's job ➤ Quality gets measured and managed ➤ Aggressive pursuit of superior results ➤ Judicious investment in Prevention and up-front Detection
Quality is a Cost Centre	Quality is a Profit Centre!

Contrary to popular belief, managing health costs is not like herding cats. With the compelling and familiar reference point of Cost of Quality, we can now revitalize our accounting for health (see Chapter 5).

Myth #4: We need Leadership "Heroes" to Save Us

> *"The only thing you take with you when you're gone is what you leave behind."*
>
> John Allston

I'm giving special attention to this next myth because, in my view, it erodes the very foundations of our efforts to build healthy and high performing organizations. Pop leadership culture would have us believe that we are dependent on passionate, visionary, enlightened leaders to "save" our organizations.

Fact:

> *"My name is Ozymandius, King of Kings,*
> *Look on my Works, ye Mighty, and despair!*
> *Nothing beside remains. Round the decay*
> *Of that colossal Wreck, boundless and bare*
> *The lone and level sands stretch far away."*
>
> Percy Bysshe Shelley
> *Ozymandius* , 1817

Hero worship is not only misguided, it can be dangerous. There are two factors, which militate against dependence on hero leaders:

- *First, the average tenure of Fortune 100 CEO's* is 3.5 years.[41] And this average is dropping fast. That doesn't leave much time to transform an organization, much less build a legacy. Not that it can't be done, but it places significant onus on our leaders of the new millennium to not only shine while they are in the driver's seat, but also to prevent the organization from tarnishing after they leave.

- *Second, hero worship breeds a perverse sort of learned helplessness* within organizations—disappointment when newly appointed leaders are not perceived to be Rain Men; and profound despair when enlightened leaders leave.

The disturbing truth is that inspirational leaders may create Nirvana in the short term, and chaos on their departure. Many an inspirational leader rolls into town, creates extraordinary transformation, and then the whole house of cards collapses when they leave.

Like footprints in the sand, wiped out by a single wave, so are the efforts of many a stellar CEO obliterated with the passing of the flame. This is even truer for their organizational health efforts, which are still deemed by many managers to be capricious frills.

Interestingly, in *Built to Last*, Collins and Porras' research on sustained high performance organizations supports my bias that charismatic leaders are more frill than necessity. In fact, the authors point to management bricks and mortar, built by self-effacing leaders, as the means by which organizations sustain values and improvements across successive leaderships.[42]

> *"The very essence of democracy is to avoid overdependence on any single leader and put the primary focus on the process... A charismatic visionary leader is absolutely not required for a visionary company and, in fact, can be detrimental to a company's long-term prospects."*
>
> Collins J.C., Porras J.I.
> *Built to Last*[43]

Collins and Porras also report extraordinary mutual commitment between CEO's and these organizations—the average CEO tenure for their visionary companies between 1806 and 1992 was 17 years![44] In organizations with this kind of staying power, the organization becomes stronger than the leader. This is a good thing.

The Leadership Legacy

Until we stop idolizing leaders who create masterpieces, but leave rubble in their wake, we won't have cracked the nut of sustainable high performance.

We need to demand that our leaders leave a legacy. And part of this legacy can be in the form of a living, breathing business case—a Healthy Scorecard that quarter-after-quarter reinforces the mantra of good leadership, good health, and great business. For leaders truly serious about winning the War for Talent, it is folly not to develop a robust business case, which proves the investment value of human capital, and locks health values into the fabric of the organization's systems, processes, and structures… long after we are gone.

THE NEW FRONTIER FOR HIGH PERFORMANCE

> *"There are countless ways of achieving greatness, but any road to achieving one's maximum potential must be built on a bedrock of respect for the individual, a commitment to excellence, and a rejection of mediocrity."*
>
> Buck Rodgers

We are facing an exciting new frontier that challenges our dearly held notions about what drives health—and high performance. For us to grab the tail of this tiger, we need to cast away our preconceptions, because they are mired in tradition, not fact. We also need to cast away our emotional attachment to arguments such as, "*Whose responsibility is employee health*", and focus instead on a win/win partnership between employees and their organizations.

> *Additional Health Myths are discussed in the Further Reading Section, at the end of this book under "Putting More Health Myths to Rest".*

Leadership Check-Up

Balanced Scorecard

1) How predictive is your Balanced Scorecard?
2) How robust are your people measures?

Readiness for change

3) How ready is your organization to pursue *superior* health and human capital results?
   a) *Are your leaders sufficiently dissatisfied with their current performance?*
   b) *Did you set BHAGs, or Big Hairy Audacious Goals[45] for employee wellbeing this year?*
   c) *Are your leaders aware of their central role in reducing stress, illness, and injury rates?*
   d) *Are your leaders excited about the improvement potential from a strategic focus on health?*

Benchmarking

4) With whom do you compare your track record in employee wellbeing? (Check all that apply).
   a) *Internal improvements over time*
   b) *World-class benchmarks*
   c) *Industry averages*

Leadership Legacy

5) What is your senior leadership team doing to leave a healthy leadership legacy for your organization?

Responsibility Rhetoric

6) What are you doing to make it *convenient* for your employees to improve their wellbeing?

3

TOP BOX RESULTS

"Increasing mean satisfaction is strategically different than increasing the percentage of delighted customers and employees."

Steve Kirn, VP, Innovation and Organization Development
Sears Roebuck and Co.[46]

RAISING THE BAR ON PERFORMANCE: TOP BOX RESULTS

Do you know what it takes to retain your employees and keep them committed? What it takes to retain your customers—or prevent them from gobbling up resources because they are disgruntled?

Your competitors do. New to your neighborhood is a new threshold in performance, called "Top Box Results". And if you don't yet know what your top box is for employee and customer outcomes, your performance results are nowhere near what they could be.

Top box results represent the level of employee and customer satisfaction where *average* business results become *superior*. But despite the hype about a global economy and pressure on our public sector organizations to be competitive, most organizations still do not differentiate "OK" survey results from great ones.

Fact is, employees and customers are getting more and more demanding. And they can afford to be. A quick look at demographics[47], the intensely competitive New Economy, and the globalization of business confirms that employees and customers are both hot items.

How far do organizations have to go to please customers? Most organizations have no clue. But the leaders and investors which explore the top box receive a rude, but necessary awakening.

Like it or not, it matters whether employees and customers are merely satisfied, delighted, or committed.[48] *But where is the threshold where it matters the most?*

Does your organization know where performance improvements make the most difference? Is the magical threshold between the 4's and 5's on a scale of 5? Is it between the 6's and 7's on a scale of 7?

Organizations such as Sears Roebuck[49], Xerox[50], Celestica[51], and the City of Calgary[52] are learning what this Maginot Line[53] is. And they are precisely calibrating their performance targets to reflect just *how* outstanding they need to be.

The new reality is that it can spell disaster for public *and* private sector organizations to pursue a melting pot of "*Mean Satisfieds*" or "*Aggregate Satisfieds*"— the full spectrum from the marginally satisfied, to the extremely satisfied zealots.[54] Even scarier, it can be fruitless to pursue very good results, when only exceptional results count for survival in this global economy.

Top box results provide more useful improvement information than a mean or aggregate satisfaction score. As Steve Kirn notes, they provide a common focus for recognition, and support managers in recognizing and rewarding truly top performers.[55]

Most importantly, top box results are the engine of superior and enduring customer and financial results. And this isn't bad news. It's great news!

The Danger of Aggregate "Satisfieds"

> *"We have found that top performers are quantifiably different from their more average counterparts."*
>
> The Gallup Organization
> *The Gallup Path to Business Outcomes*[56]

One of the best ways to pad performance results and reinforce complacency is to report the full spectrum of satisfied responses as one puréed group. From the "*Polite Dissatisfieds*" and "*Marginally Satisfieds*" to the "*Totally Satisfied*" zealots, managers are expected to derive meaning from this purée of information. Even more frightening, they are expected to act on it! Like sirens, luring the voyager Odysseus to peril, so do padded satisfaction results entice leaders to misstate reality.

Aggregate results reinforce complacency (*"85% of customers are satisfied? WOW!"*), hide significant shifts within the satisfied cadre, and stifle our ability to nimbly address performance issues. How can we possibly expect to make effective use of scarce resources, when we subsist on misleading performance results?

Cultivating top box results demands that our measurement and reporting systems keep up—and that they are honest and transparent.

No Pain, No Gain

> *The problem with top box reporting is that your initial results may look really, really bad.*

Xerox encountered this challenge, when they shifted their reporting of employee satisfaction results. In 1990 their top box employee satisfaction outcomes registered a measly 37%. But they stuck to their guns, and were able to report improvements to 77% by 1998.[57]

> *The silver lining with top-box reporting is that you set the stage for spectacular turnarounds.*

During this time, Xerox reset the target for customer satisfaction from the aggregate target of ninety percent 4's and 5's in 1990, to one hundred percent 5's in 1996.

Keep in mind that Xerox's 5's in customer satisfaction represented six times the repurchase clout of the 4's! This is the kind of information that should have shareholders leaning forward in their seats!

The Emperor's New Clothes

One organization that I encountered took another route. They thrived on their phenomenal reputation as a healthy organization. But there were significant cracks in the foundation. The story told by objective employee data was of an organization needing significant improvement. Not only were their top box results marginal, (Fig. 4), but there was also a significant gap between management and employee perceptions of how well they were doing (Fig. 3).

In other words, managers were out of touch with key employee issues.

Surprisingly, this was the first time that a gap analysis had been conducted between manager and employee opinions. It was not welcome news.

But this kind of news should be celebrated!

Any time such a gap analysis is performed between management and employee perceptions, it begs the questions, "Do managers know what the *most important* employee issues are?" "Do managers know what the *worst-performing* issues are?"

In this particular case (Fig. 3), 47% of senior managers strongly agreed that they were meaningfully involved in decisions that affected them at work. Only 12% of staff strongly agreed.

Figure 3

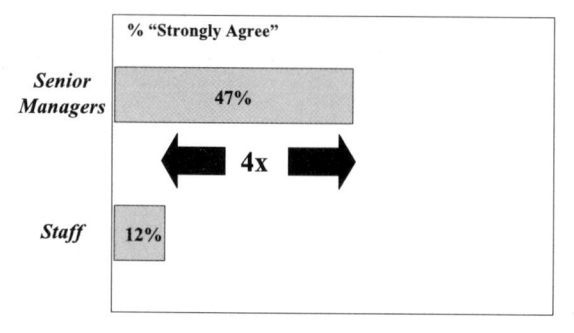

"I am meaningfully involved in decisions that affect me..."

% "Strongly Agree"

Senior Managers: 47%

⬅ 4x ➡

Staff: 12%

Source: *The identity of this organization is intentionally not revealed.*

> *"How can a leadership team define strategic priorities when their perception of reality is protected by rose-colored glasses?"*

This organization was also intent on measuring aggregate satisfaction which, not surprisingly, yielded high satisfaction results. So they began to believe their own press. After all, 81% of staff overall were satisfied that they were involved in decisions, weren't they?

Unfortunately only 12% of staff strongly agreed. (Fig. 4)

Figure 4

Staff Responses

"I am meaningfully involved in decisions that affect me..."

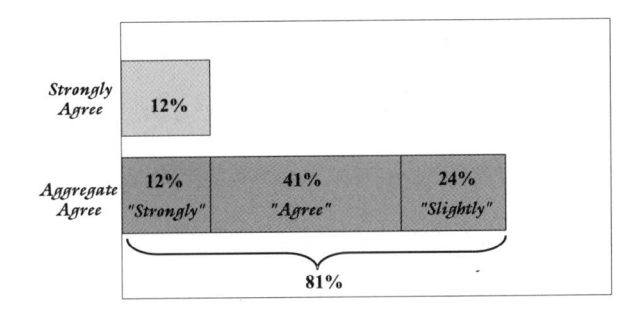

Strongly Agree	12%		
Aggregate Agree	12% "Strongly"	41% "Agree"	24% "Slightly"

81%

Source: *The identity of this organization is intentionally not revealed.*

As a small player in a cutthroat industry, this organization desperately needed a burning platform for change.

It requires leadership backbone to shift the reporting of customer or employee opinion data from the large and fuzzy "Aggregate Satisfied" bucket, to the significantly smaller "Top Bucket".

But this bold move opens up the door for meaningful and exciting performance improvements, targeted to the high-impact top box results.[58]

> *"As long as we subsist on aggregate satisfaction results, we shield ourselves from reality, stifle our ability to learn about truly high performance, and live the myth of the Emperor's New Clothes."*

Shifts within overall results are hidden

Another problem with full-spectrum reporting of "*Satisfied*" scores is that strategically significant shifts within the results can be hidden.

The City of Calgary was recognized in 1999 by the Institute of Public Administration of Canada's Award for Innovative Management, for its lead in measuring and reporting citizen survey results. Recognizing the problem inherent in aggregate reporting, the City is working to define and pursue top box results. Figure 5 illustrates that between 1997 and 1999, the City reported negligible change in citizens' *overall* satisfaction results, from 90% in 1997, to 87% in 1999. No cause for concern. Or is there?

Figure 5

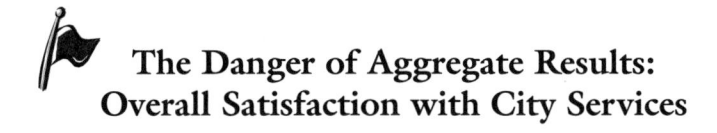

🚩 The Danger of Aggregate Results: Overall Satisfaction with City Services

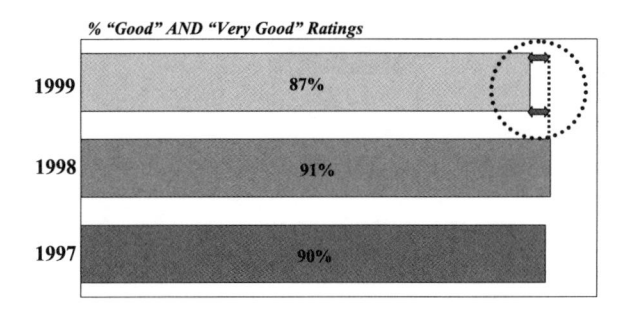

% "Good" AND "Very Good" Ratings

Year	Rating
1999	87%
1998	91%
1997	90%

Source: *City of Calgary Customer Satisfaction Survey,* Final Report, 1999.

When the results are disaggregated, a different picture presents. Concealed by these results is a halving of the "*Very Good*" representation, illustrated in Figure 6, from 52% in 1997, to 26% in 1999![59]

It is astonishing that, while the common man looks for greater resolution in TV screens and computer monitors, the average manager subsists on fuzzy, infrequent employee data. High performance organizations are noted for their agility, and for their ability to adapt quickly to change. This requires employee and customer data that is sensitive to change—something most organizations are lacking.

Until we improve the granularity of our employee—and customer—measures, we won't see change coming until it has already happened. Even worse, employees will *feel* the change, but managers won't *believe* it is happening, because the numbers tell them "all's well".

Figure 6

The Danger of Aggregate Results: Overall Satisfaction with City Services

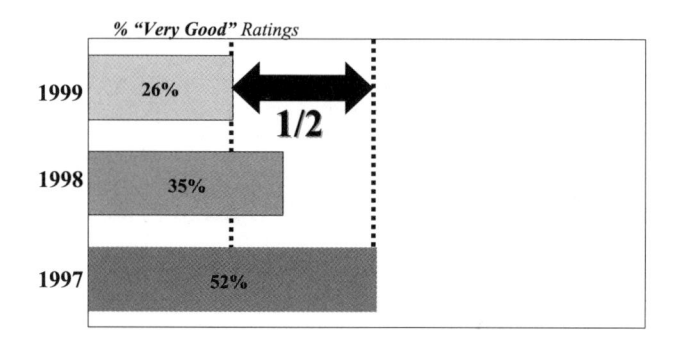

% *"Very Good"* Ratings

Year	Rating
1999	26%
1998	35%
1997	52%

1/2

Source: *City of Calgary Customer Satisfaction Survey*, Final Report, 1999.

Aggregate results are like a Trojan Horse in your workplace. They look inspiring, but hide dangers that you're better off knowing about.

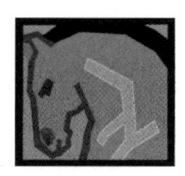

"Top Box" Customer Results

"We will deliver unsurpassed customer service."

Bank One
Five Imperatives, from *1999 Bank One Annual Report*

Let's take a closer look at why top box results matter so much. Fortunately, there is a growing cadre of organizations which embrace top-box customer results. Xerox found that customers who gave them a "*Very Satisfied*" rating were *6x more likely* to repurchase equipment than those who merely gave a "*Satisfied*" rating.[60]

Calgary Transit, found that among riders rating overall service as "*Excellent*", 66% were committed to continued use of Transit, whereas only 51% of riders giving "*Good*" and 36% of riders giving "*Satisfactory*" ratings were committed.[61] Transit use ultimately translates into reduced traffic congestion, improved air quality, and improved overall quality of life, so it is strategically important to improve rider commitment in a rapidly growing city such as Calgary. And this means targeting that top box in customer satisfaction results.

A Perfect 10

Sears Roebuck is targeting perfect 10's.

Sears has found that their biggest drop-off in customer loyalty behaviour is between the 9's and 10's on a scale of 10. (Fig. 7)

Specifically, they have found that among customers who give a 10 out of 10 on "*Overall Satisfaction*", 82% "*Definitely Would Recommend*" Sears to their friends. There is a dizzying drop when customers give a very respectable 9 out of 10: only 33% "*Definitely Would Recommend*" Sears to their friends![62]

Figure 7

Why Perfect 10's in Customer Satisfaction are Strategically Important to Sears

SEARS

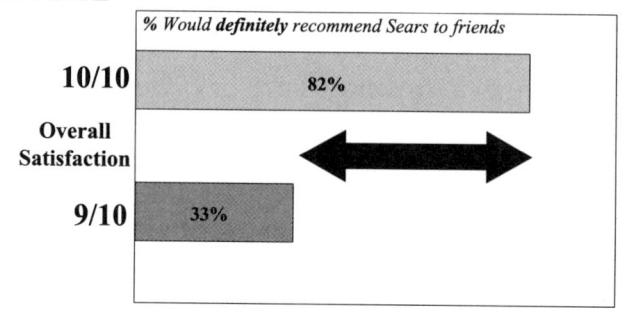

% Would **definitely** recommend Sears to friends

Overall Satisfaction
- 10/10: 82%
- 9/10: 33%

Source: Steve Kirn, VP Innovation and Organization Development, Sears Roebuck, *Embedding HR Metrics in Total Performance Indicators*, presentation to IQPC's HR Measurement Conference 2001, San Francisco.

This stomach-churning drop tells Sears executives that (supposedly) superior satisfaction results at the level of 9 out of 10 generate only mediocre customer results.

To reap the benefits of customer loyalty, Sears must WOW their customers with 10's on a scale of 10!

The research on customer loyalty is not new. One of my favorite examples of loyalty is from Frederick Reicheld, whose study on customer defection habits appeared in 1993 in the *Journal of Retail Banking*.[63] (See Figure 8). In a review of customers who had defected from another financial institution, Reicheld found that 90% of defectors had been "*Satisfied*" with their original provider!

Figure 8

% Defecting Customers "*Satisfied*" with Original Provider

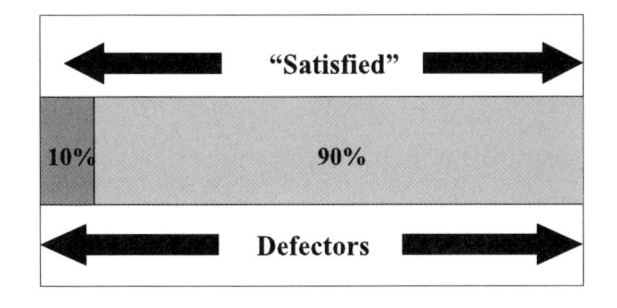

"Satisfied"	
10%	90%
Defectors	

Source: Reicheld F., Aspinwall K. Building High-Loyalty Business Systems, *Journal of Retail Banking*, Winter, 1993/94.

So when an organization like Bank One—noted for its zeal for employee-customer-profit linkages—announces a key focus on customers most likely to defect, this implies an aggressive focus on top-box results, not just satisfied customers.[64]

It's not much of a leap to conclude that superior customer results demand superior employee results.

What a way to create an appetite for cultural transformation! So it comes as no surprise that Steve Kirn, VP of Innovation and Organization Development for Sears Roebuck and Co., describes one of the cornerstones of their strategy as developing a "Winning Culture".[65]

"Top Box" Employee Results

Employee commitment is all the rage, thanks to population aging, demanding Gen X'ers, an exploding New Economy, and a War for Talent. But it needn't take this kind of brinkmanship to demand excellence in employee results. While it is arguably convenient to have these forces at play, at the end of the day, cultivating employee commitment is simply an exercise in accounting logic.

The benefits of employee commitment can be expressed in dollars—in terms of substantially reduced costs and improved service in the public sector, or dramatically increased profits in the private sector. But you've heard this before.

What you may not have heard yet is that we can now precisely measure the opportunity costs of poor wellbeing: lost quality, innovation, and productivity.

Superior customer results demand superior employee service. As Jim Clemmer once commented,

> "How can a dissatisfied, disgruntled, demoralized employee deliver high levels of customer satisfaction?"
>
> Jim Clemmer
> Executive Briefing Session
> Calgary, 1998

More to the point,

How can a stressed, ill, injured employee deliver superior levels of customer satisfaction?

Yet I can't count the number of times that executives become skittish at my mere mention of employee **delight**. "Isn't it a little over the top to use the term 'Delight' for employees?", they squirm.

In the private sector, the dazzling profit implications of top box results demand that we leverage our human capital. Whether executives are accountable to boards, shareholders, or their own wallets, the new imperative is that we unearth significant improvement opportunities. And health is a minefield of untapped opportunity!

In the public sector, taxpayers—and legislators—are also demanding greater accountability, not to mention superior performance. In the U.S., this has taken the form of the Government Performance and Results Act. Passed by Congress in 1993, the GPRA has spurred significant improvements in government accountability and results. Not surprisingly, there has been an explosion of interest in Balanced Scorecards. [66]

Competing on Culture

Culture is now seen as a competitive lever, even in the public sector. But not everyone wants in. At a recent executive workshop, a public sector manager commented to me, *"Come on, does 'employee delight' really fit in the public sector?"*. You better believe it does.

Managers that don't understand the trickle-down effect of the Brain Drain are in for a rude awakening. Just as the dot-coms are stealing employees from Big Blue… so is the private sector poaching talent from the public sector.

This is akin to the great white shark, whose natural feeding grounds have been disrupted by global over-fishing. Now great whites are found in non-traditional territory, and the locals are—quite literally—getting eaten alive.[67]

The City of Calgary recognizes that it cannot compete against the big guns in salaries. But it might compete on the basis of culture.

This perspective levels the playing field for cash-strapped organizations, and ups the *ante* for organizations serious about high performance. The City has responded to this opportunity by locking wellbeing and capability drivers into their Balanced Scorecard, and is now moving toward holding managers accountable for employee, as well as customer, process, and financial results.

Recently The Gallup Organization has enjoyed centre stage for its exciting bestseller, *"First, Break all the Rules"*. In a dazzlingly simple 12-point survey, (*The Q^{12} Advantage*®), the Gallup researchers contend they have found the elixir of employee retention and productivity! (More on this in Chapter 4). The power of these 12 questions is in the extreme wording, such as in, "At work I have the opportunity to do what I do *best every day*."

> *"We discovered that if you removed the extreme language, the question lost much of its power to discriminate (between the most productive departments and the rest)."*

The Gallup researchers go on to describe the onus on leaders to build not only accountability for results, but also capability to deliver top box results.

> *"Perhaps the best thing any leader can do to drive the whole company toward greatness is, first, to hold each manager accountable for what his employees say to these twelve questions, and second, to help each manager know what actions to take to deserve 'Strongly Agree' responses from his employees."*
>
> Buckingham M., Coffman C.
First, Break all the Rules! [68]

For organizations serious about high performance, the new mantra for customer and employee results is, *"Go big or stay home."*

TOWARD STAKEHOLDER BALANCE

The paradigm that I like to use to describe a healthy organization is that of *sustainable* high performance. This balanced stakeholder approach maximizes results for shareholders, customers, employees, and the organization.

But for organizations to reach this Nirvana, they need to first stomach the notion of employee delight—and then master the art of *simultaneously* climbing up the ladders of customer and employee delight. This is easier said than done.

The Penal Colony

Legions of workplaces have proven that it feels far easier to have tunnel vision. The old "2x4" school of management would have us believe that employees are out to cheat the company, and that we need to just beat them into submission to get results.

To be fair, this works. But only to a point.

Penal Colony organizations excel at aggressively pursuing customer delight… at the expense of employees. They are often admired for their military approach to process and customer improvements, and their cavalier "tow the line" approach to employees. In the name of short term—and might I add fleeting—shareholder return, legions of organizations pursue mergers and acquisitions while focusing on organizational structure, not people. And while such Penal Colony workplaces are often led under the guise of prudent financial management, the reality reflects dated, sloppy, myopic accounting.

Performance in these organizations is fragile. Witness the number of high performance organizations and teams which fizzle… or the roaring churn in the high tech industry, notorious for chewing up employees and spitting them out. Even the dot-coms have their Icarus:[69]

> *"If, for example, Value America had spent less on advertising ($69 million in 1999 on a revenue base of $183 million) and invested even half that in assembling an army of the best possible people, then perhaps it would have avoided the distinction of becoming the consummate dot-com implosion."*
>
> James C. Collins
> *Business Week*[70]

Penal Colony workplaces are in for a rough ride when the demanding Gen X'ers enter the workforce in 2005. But there's hope for a turnaround, particularly if these organizations can stay on familiar turf, and view health capital as an accounting improvement.

The Country Club

Another recipe for disaster is the Country Club organization, which single-mindedly pursues employee delight. These organizations also have tunnel vision. Their definition of success misses the need for sustainable business results.

One of W. Edwards Deming's key quality values was "pride of workmanship."[71] The Country Club organizations miss out on this deep sense of purpose which arises from operational excellence, and a well-executed organizational mission.

> *"Remove barriers which rob the... worker of his right to pride of workmanship."*
>
> Deming W.E.,
> *14 Points for Management*[72]

So while Country Club organizations make life cushy, they may not necessarily make it cushy where it counts. These organizations do the greatest disservice possible to their employees—they go out of business. Witness the roadkill for the early winners on the *"Best Places to Work For"* highway.

The Penal Club

Even worse is the Penal Colony-Country Club—the organizations which *force* health and happiness on their people. These workplaces are typically led by fundamentalist health zealots who arrogantly decree what is best for employees. In these organizations, the leaders take great pride in having a "healthy workplace". They point to the superficial trappings of a healthy lifestyle: healthy food in the cafeteria, shiny equipment in the fitness room, and possibly job screening which filters out "undesirables". They might even decree a no-conflict zone, where employees are penalized for openly voicing their opinions. And yet constructive dissent is at the heart of learning.

> *"All men have an instinct for conflict:*
> *at least, all healthy men."*
>
> Hilaire Belloc
> *The Silence of the Sea*[73]

The morale in these organizations tells a different story. Like the eerie "happiness" of the townsfolk in the movie *Pleasantville*[74], the culture in these Penal Clubs is throbbingly toxic. Employee wellbeing is coerced, and misses the lifeblood of organizational justice, freedom of choice, and support to make enlightened decisions.

Some years ago, in consulting to a large health care organization in Canada, one of the senior managers begged me,

> *"Please don't take away the fries in our cafeteria...*
> *they're the only source of light*
> *in this place."*

Leaders who merely purge junk food from their workplaces, or who force time-starved employees to attend social events on their personal time, in an effort to make the place healthier, are entirely missing the point. So it comes as a refreshing breeze to come across more flexible definitions of wellbeing, such as that of Harry Rosen, clothing magnate:

> *"Rubbish videos, a daily workout,*
> *and only the occasional shot of (100 proof) vodka."*
>
> Harry Rosen
> *MacLean's Magazine*[75]

or the perspective of Ricardo Semler, Brazilian CEO extraordinaire,

> "...you won't find a running track or swimming pool or gym at Semco. Many companies build them to help their employees cope with stress... we try not to cause stress in the first place."
>
> Ricardo Semler
> Maverick[76]

The true measure of a healthy organization is not in its programs, but in its *feel*: its ability to foster both employee and customer delight, in the pursuit of high performance.

SUSTAINABLE HIGH PERFORMANCE

> "What distinguished the unusually successful companies from their competitors was a measurable advantage in customer and employee loyalty. Each time we found a performance record that was hard to square with the traditional economics taught in business schools, we also found a company with superior loyalty... that was delivering superior value to its customers and employees, and at the same time delivering inexplicably strong cash flows..."
>
> F. F. Reichheld,
> The Loyalty Effect[77]

And then in the balance we find organizations which aggressively pursue both employee and customer delight. These organizations get it. They judiciously balance the needs of employees and customers—and in doing so create the conditions for enduring and superior performance results. Leaders in these workplaces recognize that employee and customer results are not an either/or proposition… and that employee and customer satisfaction feed off each other. So they climb both ladders of customer and employee delight.

The Satisfaction Mirror

> "Rocket science is not required
> to explain the satisfaction mirror."
>
> Heskett J.L., Sasser W.E., Schlesinger L.A.,
> *The Service Profit Chain*, 1997

In their luminous book *The Service Profit Chain*, James Heskett, Leonard Schlesinger, and Earl Sasser write about the *"Satisfaction Mirror"*, the powerful synergy between employer and customer satisfaction.[78] Their high-octane research captures not only the spiral of goodwill which arises from satisfied customers and employees, but also the economies gained when satisfied employees serve satisfied and loyal customers. This team's work elegantly captures how improved customer satisfaction yields the golden nugget of customer complaints.

As customers become more satisfied, they become more comfortable making complaints.

This in turn reveals untapped opportunities for performance improvement.

Figure 9

The Satisfaction Mirror

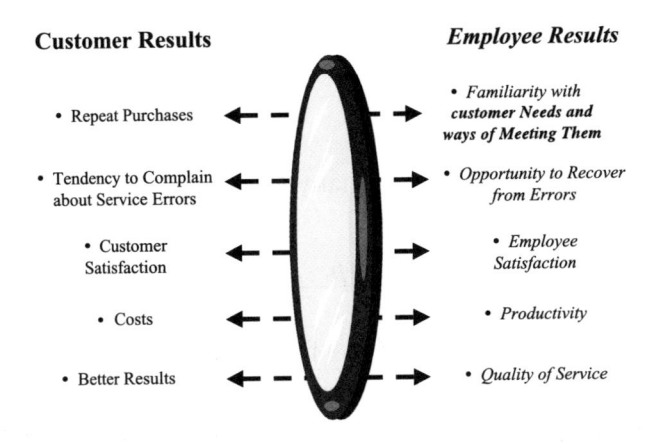

Customer Results
- Repeat Purchases
- Tendency to Complain about Service Errors
- Customer Satisfaction
- Costs
- Better Results

Employee Results
- *Familiarity with customer Needs and ways of Meeting Them*
- *Opportunity to Recover from Errors*
- *Employee Satisfaction*
- *Productivity*
- *Quality of Service*

Source: Heskett *et al.*, *The Service Profit Chain*. 1997. Reproduced with permission from the authors.

Strategic Health Focus: The Missing Rungs

But there is trouble in paradise. Because there are rungs missing on the ladder of employee capability and delight. The problem is that any serious pursuit of top-box employee results requires that leaders understand what motivates—and hinders—human performance. And this inevitably leads us to the drivers of employee wellbeing.

Organizations truly serious about top box employee results, must understand what drives stress, illness, and injury.

With the best of intentions, many leaders go astray here.

Wellbeing Programs: Comprehensive but not Strategic

One of the ways leaders fall off the ladder is by delegating employee wellbeing to clinical experts. This arms-length relationship with wellbeing often results in a dizzying array of wellness programs, such as smoking cessation, physical fitness, flexible work options, financial planning, and eldercare. A quick browse through *Fast Company*, *Fortune*, or the *Financial Post's Best Companies to Work For* features gives us a taste of these hot offerings.

To be fair, these wellness programs are often quite impressive, covering the spectrum from:

- ***Prevention to management*** of stress/illness/injury;
- ***On-the-job and off-the-job*** risk management;
- ***Employee and family*** services;
- ***Short and Long-Term Disability***, Worker's Compensation, and Return-to-Work.

Typically missing are the cultural glue, the values stated and lived, the clearly articulated vision, the metrics and the alignment to hold these programs together. If the road gets rocky, and times get tough, these initiatives are the first to get the axe. In short, comprehensive health focus is not the same as Strategic Health Focus.

The Inspired Leader: Strategic Health Focus

> *"...we have declared war on accidents in our workplace... We can best demonstrate our commitment to our employees by sending them home to their family healthy and whole. A safe place to work is a right that belongs to everyone, and it must always be our first priority."*
>
> Tom Stephens
> *Speech to 1998 Annual General Meeting*
> MacMillan Bloedel Ltd.

Spectacular turnarounds in employee wellbeing can be achieved when an inspired leader takes the helm. Witness the 10-fold reduction in lost time injuries, and the 25-fold reduction in lost-time days between 1990 and 1993, when Ted Pattenden took the helm at NRI Industries Inc. Or the 56% reduction in Medical Incidences Reportable between 1997 and 1999 at MacMillan Bloedel, when Tom Stephens, acclaimed turnaround artiste, became CEO.

When it comes to health and safety, passionate leaders get things done. Leaders that are passionate about employee wellbeing allocate budgets, define accountabilities, and put health and safety high on the executive agenda. When Tom Stephens took the helm at the former MacMillan Bloedel (now Weyerhaeuser), he made safety a top priority. He seconded employees from front-line jobs and created safety "SWAT-teams" which combed the organization for safety improvements. He openly cited audacious safety goals to the media.[79] And he got results.

But what happens when the enlightened leader leaves? Will the whole house of cards collapse? Far too often, it does.[80]

The Sustainable Strategic Health Focus

The leaders that really turn my crank are the ones which build *staying power* for health and safety values. While short-term results from a new CEO are exciting, the true measure of a leader's success is whether health and safety improvements are sustained after the CEO's departure.

Tom Carson, Deputy Minister of Health for Manitoba, Canada, and a leading thinker on organizational health, agrees that we are on thin ice. [81] Until we build a living business case—and lock health values into our workplaces, we run the very real risk that wellness is simply a "flavor of the CEO". Small consolation when we're dealing with an average Fortune 100 CEO tenure of 3.5 years.[82]

So what on earth are we doing when we applaud short-term wellness results? Wellness advocates are as much to blame as employees and managers. It's high time that we become more sophisticated consumers, and demand that spectacular results also be sustainable.

In the groundbreaking book *"Built to Last"*, authors James Collins and Jerry Porras test our assumptions that enduring organizational success depends on flashy leadership. If anything, the reverse appears to be true. In the companies with staying power, the organization is clearly greater than its leaders. In fact, many of the organizations featured in *"Built to Last"* are characterized by plodding leaders, and decidedly unsexy (but robust) management systems. Clearly, leadership fortitude is required to set up robust management systems in the first place. But once health and safety are built into the organization, we are less affected by leadership churn.

*It's time that we evaluate leaders
on their "stick rate" for
strategic health improvements,
not just their initial splash-effect.*

It is not enough for us to create healthy organizations today. Let's not just build castles in the sand, but also sustainability for tomorrow.

LEADERSHIP CHECK-UP

Top Box Employee Results

1) Does your leadership team squirm if you mention the words "*employee delight*"?
2) Do you measure your success on the basis of "*Satisfied*" employees, or "*Top Box*" results?
3) What is your organization's Top Box for employee results?
4) Are you prepared to disclose just how small your Top Box is?
5) To what extent are Top Box employee results rewarded?

Sustainable Health Focus

6) What are you doing to build sustainability for your health/safety values?
7) What would happen to your organization's health/safety results if you left your job tomorrow? One year from now, would they be:

   a) Better?

   b) No change?

   c) Worse?

   d) Not sure?

4

Good Health is Good Leadership

Looking for Health in all the Wrong Places

The Trouble with Benchmarking

Benchmarking, we are told, will add high octane to the learning curve. You can shorten your learning cycle. Accelerate improvement efforts. Save time and make money. But benchmarking can blow up in your face if you mimic the wrong things.

For years, our leaders—with the best of intentions—have doomed us to mediocre performance, by accepting a narrow and traditional definition of health.

Specifically, we've been lured by programs—such as health care, disability management, stress management, and lifestyle interventions—while the toxic brew of leadership culture that drives event and severity rates has been overlooked.

In fairness to the medical establishment, many health professionals have never been exposed to the leadership-health link. And this lack of awareness permeates the highest levels of the health establishment:

> **The C. Everett Koop National Health Awards.** In the U.S., the esteemed Koop Awards, the *crème de la crème* of corporate health awards, are acclaimed for their scientific rigor. Yet they almost exclusively focus on personal health habits and cost-effective use of health care services.[83] In doing so, the Koops miss the engine of truly superior workplace health outcomes: cultural interventions.

> **The Globe and Mail, Canada.** In a recent cover story entitled, "Getting Health Care's Priorities Straight", Canada's *Globe and Mail*[84] blithely reported that, "*in a world of shifting (health) costs, there cannot be sustainability*". This kind of argument flies in the face of logic, if not basic supply-and-demand economics. The inference is that we can't do anything about the demand for health services. While I do support enlightened health system investments, we can also exert dramatic influence

on the demand for health services, through effective prevention and informed consumerism. Yet this demand reduction argument is sadly lacking from the health establishment.

- *The Canadian Medical Association.* The leaders of our health establishments are also prey to this myopia. In his address to the Annual General Meeting of the Canadian Medical Association, the newly elected president commented on the *"four key elements of sustainability"* for the Canadian health care system. Not one of these mentioned prevention, despite the fact that an enlightened leadership culture can chop stress, illness, and injury rates at least by half![85]

The powers that be have a major awareness gap.

> *Our approach to workplace health is broken, but our powerbrokers don't know that they don't know how to fix it.*

We need a paradigm shift from the medical model to the leadership model.

The Offensive Play: Reducing Event Rates

I remember being captivated by Davis Sheremata's tale of how Canadian hailstorms are rendered impotent by cloud seeding.[86] Intrepid pilots fly into the core of a hail cloud, and seed it with silver iodide. Like Viagra in reverse, the hailstones get smaller, and damage on the ground is minimized. Not surprisingly, the Alberta insurance industry views hail-busting as prudent risk management. They provide $7.5 million a year for cloud seeding to prevent the kind of $350 million payout they experienced in 1991.

Many leaders are simply overwhelmed by the barrage of health costs that rain down on their organization. When you're in this state of paralysis, a defensive approach of cost containment is an understandable reaction. But as anyone in competitive sports will attest, when you're losing badly, more stiff-upper-lip defensive play just doesn't cut it. You need an offensive strategy.

If we reduce the *event* rate for stress, illness, and injury, and not only the *cost per event*, we reduce our vulnerability to health cost inflation. But we stand no chance to stop the health cost downpour if we rely on a finger-in-the-dike strategy.

Begin with the End in Mind

A few years ago I was commissioned by Health Canada to conduct a national review of comprehensive health promotion programs, and North American workplace health awards. As the results came in, it became clear to my colleague Sue Hills[87] and me, that *doing* workplace health is not the same as *being* a healthy workplace.

Rather than looking for workplaces that were doing health, we turned our attention to, "*Who's getting the best health outcomes?*"—without making assumptions about how these outcomes were achieved.

Join me now as we explore companies with the best health outcomes, to find out "*How did they do it?*"!

A New Paradigm for Health

> *"...it seemed to us that inability to deliver results to customers was the number one source of frustration to frontline service employees."*
>
> James Heskett, Earl Sasser, Leonard Schlesinger
> *The Service Profit Chain*[88]

There is a new paradigm for how we look at organizational health, and this requires that we understand the determinants of health and safety, *as well as* those of high performance. Allow me to share a few of my favorite research examples ...

Research Highlights: The Healthiest Companies

Stress-Busting

The Northwestern National Life Study

The health insurance industry is understandably fascinated with what produces health costs. A select group of insurers has contributed substantially to our understanding of health, by studying the characteristics of their best group-benefit clients.

In 1991 and 1992, Northwestern National Life (NWNL) produced a series of studies on job stress.[89] The finding from some 26,000 employees was that organizations which actively work to prevent workers' stress, experience *less than half* the incidence of burnout, absenteeism, and related health care utilization of other organizations.

Figure 10 shows the striking impact which humanistic leadership has on stress-related illness. According to Northwestern

National Life, three key features of the low-stress workplaces are: effective communication; job discretion, or control over how work is organized; and work/life balance.

Figure 10

Management Practices and Stress-Related Illness

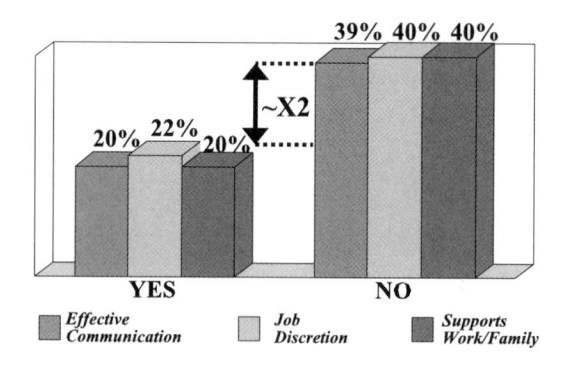

	Effective Communication	Job Discretion	Supports Work/Family
YES	20%	22%	20%
NO	39%	40%	40%

~X2

Source: NWNL Research Report, 1992.

Northwestern National Life released a list of key actions that their best group benefit clients took. These include:

- Improve *communication*
- Reduce *personal conflicts*
- Give adequate *control*
- Ensure adequate staffing/expense budgets (or *re-prioritize work* to reflect tighter budgets)

- *Recognize/reward* employees; and
- Reduce *red tape.*

"Workers Under Pressure"

In 1992, the St. Paul's Fire and Marine Insurance Company released its *Workers Under Pressure* study.[90] This highly acclaimed study of 28,000 workers emphasized the role of organizational culture and management practices in preventing stress. The study recommended that the first step in reducing workplace health event rates and costs be to identify and remove unnecessary major work stressors. Key stress abatement strategies included:

- Improving *supervisory skills* and work group relationships;
- Reducing *unnecessary work*;
- Ensuring *fair employment* and work practices; and
- Setting *"family-friendly"* policies to facilitate balance.

While organizations have traditionally emphasized stress *management*, the emerging focus includes stress *abatement*, cutting off negative stress at the source.

Sounds like motherhood and apple pie? Read on…

Disability Prevention

Columbia School of Business Study

And then in 1995, Unum Insurance Company commissioned the Columbia School of business to do a report on 700,000 employees, entitled *"The Determinates and Consequences of Workplace Disability"*. The researchers found that human resources practices profoundly impact sickness and disability rates. Foremost among these were:

- "The degree of *employee involvement* and participation in work decisions.
- The extent and use of *conflict management*, dispute resolution and grievance procedures.[91]
- *Workforce stabilization* and continuity policies."[92]

The researchers captured employee involvement and conflict resolution in concise indices which can serve as leading indicators of employee productivity.

Work Organization

The National Institute of Occupational Safety and Health

The emerging and fertile field of "Work Organization" provides important traction for our efforts to improve workplace health and organizational performance. Under the National Occupational Research Agenda (NORA), the National Institute of Occupational Safety and Health (NIOSH) has targeted "Work Organization", or the way work processes are structured and managed, as a key frontier for significant improvement in health. NORA defines Work Organization to include:

- *Work scheduling* (e.g. work-rest schedules, hours of work and shift work);
- *Job design* (e.g. task complexity, skill and effort required, and degree of worker control);
- *Interpersonal aspects* of work (e.g. relationships with supervisors and coworkers);
- *Career concerns* (e.g. job security and growth opportunities);
- *Management style* (e.g. participatory management practices and teamwork); and
- *Organizational characteristics* (e.g. climate, culture, and communications).[93]

The research on Work Organization reads like a shopping list for employee retention!

In fact, Harvard's upcoming book on the *HR Scorecard* lists work organization as a key driver of "Human Capital Deliverable". In a Balanced Scorecard Collaborative NetConference, authors Dr. Brian Becker and Dr. Mark Huselid outlined the synergy between employee competencies, motivation, and work organization in generating "Human Capital Deliverable".[94] (Fig. 11)

Figure 11

Putting "Work Organization" into the Strategy Map

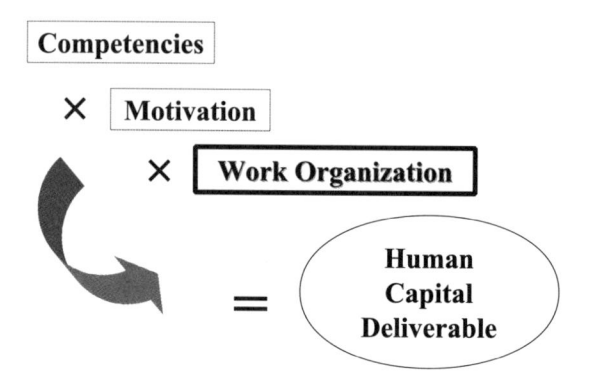

Competencies
× Motivation
× Work Organization
= Human Capital Deliverable

Copyright the Balanced Scorecard Collaborative 2000.
Source: Becker B., Huselid M., *The HR Scorecard*. Balanced Scorecard Collaborative NetConference, September 2000. Reproduced with permission from the authors.

According to NORA, if you are having problems with Work Organization, you can expect not only higher job stress, but also substantially higher injury rates. For example, you can expect to experience significantly more arm injuries (upper extremity musculoskeletal disorders) if your workplace has problems with:

➢ *Job dissatisfaction*
➢ Intensified *workload*
➢ *Monotonous* work
➢ Job *control*
➢ Job *clarity*, and
➢ Social *support*.[95][96]

Once again, leadership plays a big role in driving stress, illness and injury rates up—or down. In a publication entitled, "*Stress at Work*",[97] the National Institute for Occupational Safety and Health puts forth the following key strategies to prevent workplace stress:

- *Align workloads* with worker's capabilities and resources
- Design *stimulating, meaningful jobs*
- Define *workers' roles* and responsibilities clearly
- Give workers the opportunity to *participate in decisions* about their jobs
- Improve *communications*
- Provide opportunities for *social interaction* among workers; and
- Establish *work schedules* that are compatible with demands and responsibilities outside the job.[98]

Pioneers in Healthy Work

Whitehall I and II

There are a few studies which have shattered our preconceptions about what produces health. A landmark research project was Whitehall I, a longitudinal study begun in the 1960's, and conducted on 10,000 British civil servants. This study revealed that health and morbidity outcomes in this population were stratified by job rank. When factors such as blood pressure, smoking and cholesterol were controlled, there was still a *threefold* difference in heart disease between front-line clerical and senior executive positions! In other words:

If all job levels lived a healthy lifestyle, there would still be a three-fold difference in heart disease between the lower job ranks and the upper echelons!

The Whitehall II study was begun in 1985 to explore this difference. Dr. Michael Marmot's team of researchers at the International Centre for Health and Society (University College, London) re-examined the unexplained factors and teased out job control as the culprit.[99] In fact, the researchers found that job control had a higher explanatory power than individual coronary heart disease risk factors, such as smoking and diet!

Karasek and Theorell

Any summary of the research on healthy organizations would be incomplete without reference to the pioneering work of Drs. Robert Karasek and Töres Theorell. These luminaries uncovered new ground in 1990 with their book, *"Healthy Work: Stress, Productivity, and the Reconstruction of Working Life"*.[100] At the heart of their work is the "Demand/Control" model, which illuminates the impact of leadership on health outcomes.

The Demand/Control Model

Employees who have high demands placed on them, but little control, or decision latitude over how they meet these demands, experience dramatically higher adverse health outcomes. The technical term for this brew is Job Strain.

Figure 12

The Demand/Control Model

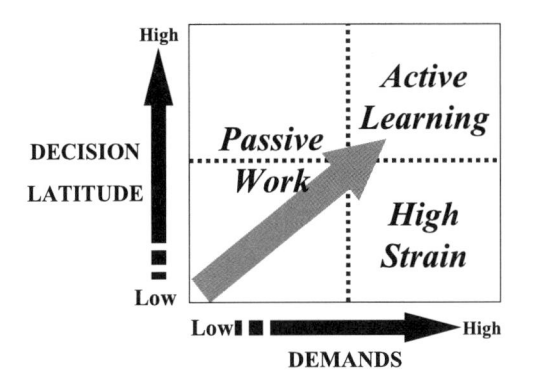

```
High
 ▲                    ┊  Active
 │         Passive    ┊  Learning
DECISION     Work  ┄┄┄┼┄┄┄┄┄┄┄┄
LATITUDE             ┊   High
                     ┊   Strain
 Low
      Low ■━━━━━━━━━▶ High
              DEMANDS
```

Source: Karasek, Theorell. *Healthy Work*, 1990.
Reprinted with permission from the authors.

The classic example of a high strain job is a teller in a complaints department, who must go through multiple levels of bureaucracy to address the needs of irate customers. This employee experiences high psychological demands, but little control over how work is done. This scenario represents a chamber of horrors for health outcomes, not to mention for customer satisfaction.

Conversely, the high control/high demand job is an incubator for learning and self-esteem. Give employees the control they need to do their job, and challenging work, and they thrive...provided the demands are not excessive. This presents a captivating parallel with W.E. Deming's position that we must facilitate pride of workmanship for our employees, and that intellectual challenge is an important part of quality improvement.[101] People don't just want a job. They want satisfying, meaningful work. This also dovetails nicely with Jim Collins' assertion that freedom of choice is a fundamental component of high performance.[102] And with Dr. Martin Shain's assertion that fairness, or organizational justice is really what health is all about. [103]

But boredom is a health risk too. Witness the mind-numbing boredom of security personnel who must stare at a bank of unmoving screens on the night shift. These jobs are characterized by low psychological demands, yet poor health outcomes. And this is why job enrichment is so important to improving employee retention in such jobs.

Strain Inhibits Learning/ Learning Inhibits Strain

> *It should come as no surprise that learning isn't just good for business— it's good for your health.*

Learning actually reduces strain by increasing an employee's sense of mastery and self-esteem. Improve the capability of your workforce, and they become more resilient to strain! Conversely, strain inhibits learning by removing the desire for risk-taking. [104] It also deprives you of REM sleep, which is vital when you're learning complex tasks.[105] In fact the latest medical research has uncovered actual physical changes in the brain, including nerve cell shrinkage and nerve cell death, resulting from low control work environments, which are associated with poor memory and loss of creativity.[106]

As my esteemed colleague Dr. Martin Shain notes,

> ... it is now clear that management practices that foster low control among employees contribute not only to illness but also to the defeat of those very skills that organizations need among their workforces to deal with the onslaught of relentless change characterizing the modern workplace.[107]

So on the one hand we hear the chorus from high performance experts, such as the Baldridge National Quality Program—exhorting us to encourage risk-taking. And now we learn that we can facilitate risk-taking if we reduce strain—and the combination of high demands/low control—which produces it. Another example of how a deeper understanding of employee health can strengthen our approach to people quality, and high performance.

I am reminded of a story about when the Iron Curtain came down. As Germany was reunited, East German workers flocked to the West. Western managers were stymied by the failure of their participative leadership style to produce results with these new employees. Innovation and the risk-taking inherent in learning were far too threatening for the East German worker, accustomed to a keep-your-head-down approach in the workplace. This was simply prudent risk management on the part of the East German worker.[108]

The Effort/Reward Imbalance Model

Another major dynamic which drives health outcomes is the balance between Effort and Reward. Töres Theorell is Director of the Karolinska Institute, Division of Psychosocial Factors and Health. His research indicates that employees who feel their efforts are not rewarded, experience dramatically higher stress, illness, and injury rates. We're not just talking about money here... we're talking about psychic pay.[109]

As the gap grows between efforts expended on a job and perceived rewards/recognition, so do health problems worsen.

Organizations with a high effort/reward gap are not just unhealthy, they are misaligned.

No wonder that Drs. Kaplan and Norton cite the biggest CEO challenge as being *implementation* of corporate strategy. In fact, Dr. Kaplan shared at a recent International Quality and Productivity Centre conference, that one of the top four barriers to strategic success is that typically only 25% of managers have their incentives linked to strategy![110] How can we ensure everyone is pulling in the same direction, when rewards and recognition are not aligned with desired behaviors?

Job Control and Canadian Public Executives

More support for the Demand/Control model comes from Dr. Wayne Corneil of Health Canada, Dr. Julian Barling of the Queen's University School of Business, and the Association of Professional Executives of the Public Service of Canada (APEX). Together, they completed in 1997 a report entitled, *Work Habits, Working Conditions, and the Health Status of the Executive Cadre in the Public Service of Canada*.[111]

The prevalence of health problems in the executive cadre is staggering. This report found that 92% percent of executives report sleep problems; 52% report stomach (GI) problems; 19% report back problems; and 16% report heart problems (Fig. 13). Not surprisingly, the researchers found that distress, health problems, and work satisfaction are tightly related.

Figure 13

Prevalence of Health Problems
% of Executives Reporting Problems

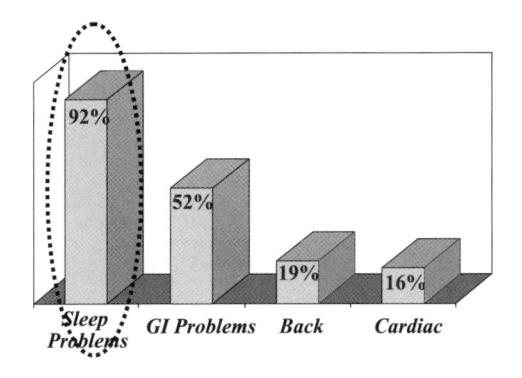

- Sleep Problems: 92%
- GI Problems: 52%
- Back: 19%
- Cardiac: 16%

Source: Corneil W., Barling J. *Work Habits, Working Conditions, and the Health of the Executive Cadre in the Public Service of Canada*: A Synopsis of APEX's 1997 Study. Association of Professional Executives of the Public Service of Canada, 1997.
Reproduced with permission from the authors.

The APEX findings point to job *control* as the strongest mediator of work stress.

> "...individuals' lack of job control is more strongly related to distress levels, short-term health complaints and longer term health disorders than other factors, including personal lifestyle habits."
>
> Wayne Corneil, Julian Barling,
> *Work Habits, Working Conditions, and the Health of the Executive Cadre in the Public Service of Canada*[112]

Specifically, the researchers found that when executives reported high job control, they experienced dramatically lower role conflict, job insecurity, and perceptions of high workload.[113]

Employees with low control reported high levels of distress. And high levels of distress were associated with dramatically worse health outcomes:

- *Musculoskeletal problems* increased by 90%
- *Cardiovascular disease* increased by 120%
- *Gastrointestinal problems* increased by 210%; and
- *Coronary heart disease* increased by 350%.

The clincher to this study was a whopping 1740% increase in mental health disorders associated with high levels of distress, and low job control.

What does this work tell us? It tells us that decision latitude, job control, or empowerment, play a massive role in producing health outcomes. Not surprisingly, the APEX researchers urge the Public Service of Canada to target improvements specifically to job control.

The Dark Side of Empowerment

But there's a rumbling that empowerment isn't all it's cracked up to be. Witness the chaos unleashed when employees are magically empowered, or even the stress which results directly from empowerment.

I am reminded of a legend from a shiny new Saturn organization.[114] As the story goes, in the first year, Saturn experienced a skyrocketing in the Employee Assistance Program utilization. Although employees were working in a brand new plant, with the best Japanese, European, and North American management techniques, the best managers, and the best employees, stress was out of control. Asked why employees were stressed, they responded it was the stress of empowerment!

Fact is, employees lacked the skills to be empowered. The next year, Saturn invested heavily in skill development for meeting management, conflict resolution and problem solving skills, and the stress levels subsided.

MDS Nordion, a winner of the National Quality Institute's Healthy Workplace Award in Canada understands this dynamic, and provides basic training to employees in problem-solving, conflict resolution, and meeting management.[115] This basic skill-building isn't just good for productive working relations—it profoundly improves health outcomes, and also prevents violence.

In discussing Nordion's approach with Gerry Smith, author of *Work Rage*[116], at a recent Conference Board of Canada function, he noted, *"If more companies did what Nordion does to equip employees to communicate and handle conflicts, we wouldn't have a violence issue between employees".*[117]

In other words, as employee capability to handle constructive dissent increases, the capacity for problem-solving increases, and the potential for violence diminishes.

World Health Organization and Safety

There is also a strong linkage between leadership and safety. In the mid-1990's, the World Health Organization (WHO) noted that among the Western industrialized nations, corporate safety performance was plateauing. But a handful of organizations were breaking through this plateau and achieving stellar results. And these organizations were differentiated by a culture of *empowerment*. [118]

A brief glance at the average safety performance of the Worker's Compensation Boards across Canada and the U.S., supports the WHO's findings that safety improvements are plateauing. On average, over the past decade, average Lost Time Injuries (LTI) per 100 employees in the U.S. and Canada have decreased marginally. Figures for the Worker's Compensation Board—Alberta confirm this story. In 1995 the lost time injury frequency was 3.5. This declined to a low-point of 3.2 in 1999, a 5-year *cumulative* improvement of 8%—hardly a turnaround.[119]

How Culture Affects Safety

> *"...businesses need to recognize that they play a major role when it comes to cutting Worker's Compensation costs, which are significantly influenced by motivational issues within the workplace."*
>
> L.D. Sukay
> Risk Management[120]

So how does culture affect safety results? My favorite example is that of National Rubber Inc., a medium-sized manufacturing company in Ontario, Canada. When Ted Pattenden assumed the helm in the early 90's, he set about to transform an ailing company on the brink of bankruptcy, to a thriving organization. Facing a massive Worker's Compensation penalty for the company's horrendous safety record, he determined to turn around the safety record (and thereby cash flow)—and the hearts of his employees—as his first priority.

Now National Rubber, apart from having an unfortunate name,[121] also faced the challenge of having five major languages—none of them English. By investing in literacy development, focusing on improving 360-degree communication, building trust that change would happen, and constantly repeating his safety mantra *("Who wants to get hurt today?")*, Ted was able to achieve a spectacular turnaround in safety, and business performance.[122]

To illustrate the impact of communication and trust on safety at National Rubber, I'll share the story of Linnett, one of Ted's many line employees, whose job it was to separate large sheets of hot, sticky rubber.

As someone who has worked onsite as the industrial Physiotherapist at a poultry processing plant, I can attest to the kind of musculoskeletal carnage which results from repeated, high-strain movements.

As the communication silos were broken down at National Rubber, Linnett and her supervisor, Rosalina, took it upon themselves to speak to the technical people responsible for the composition of the rubber: *"Can't we make this rubber less sticky?"* The result of a trusting work culture at National Rubber was a dramatic and rapid reduction in lost time injuries:

➤ A **25x** reduction in lost time days in 3 years; and
➤ A **10x** reduction in lost time injuries.

During this period, NRI's profit picture improved dramatically.[123]

Figure 14

Turnarounds in Injury Rates: How Communication Improves Safety

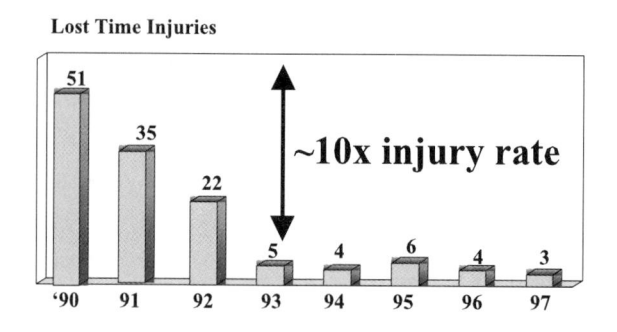

Lost Time Injuries

'90	91	92	93	94	95	96	97
51	35	22	5	4	6	4	3

~10x injury rate

Source: Personal communication, Dr. Jim Stewart, Executive-in-Residence, University of Toronto, 1966 and Ted Pattenden, CEO, NRI, 2,000.

Ted credits this profit/safety turnaround to the following philosophy:

> *"Leadership is about people, and people who believe that executives really care about what happens to them will be more likely to follow when other initiatives arise...*
>
> *Reducing injuries is a visible accomplishment which affects everyone, and one which employees genuinely appreciate."*
>
> Ted Pattenden, CEO, NRI Industries Inc.
> *Speech to OSH Safety Conference*, 1994

Ted emphasizes that employees need to have proof that their concerns will be taken seriously and addressed. It is too much to expect employees to be "empowered" when they don't believe that their feedback will be acted upon. So it was evidence of a profound cultural turnaround that Linnett and Rosalina even *bothered* to speak to the technical people about the stickiness of the rubber. And this boiled down to trust that change was possible.

Dr. Harry Shannon, researcher at Canada's Institute for Work and Health, conducted a global review of research linking management practices and injury rates. His research supports the experience at NRI Industries—the lowest injury rates are consistently associated with a participative, empowered work culture.[124]

Instilling a Sense of Community

We have known intuitively for centuries that social support is a cornerstone of wellbeing.[125] In a riveting account of the true Moby Dick story, researcher extraordinaire Nathaniel Philbrick tells of the huge impact on the survivors in a small whaling boat, when social contact is lost with their shipmates, after the ship is rammed and sunk by an enraged sperm whale.

> *"We had lost the cheering*
> *of each other's faces,*
> *that, which strange as it is,*
> *we so much required in*
> *both our mental and*
> *bodily distresses."*
>
> Nathaniel Philbrick,
> *In the Heart of the Sea;*
> *The Tragedy of the Whaleship Essex*[126]

Perhaps the most compelling evidence on the link between social support and health is in the form of an analogy. Reporting on this research, the Conference Board of Canada notes:[127]

The link between social support and health is stronger than the link between smoking and lung cancer.

So what relevance does social support have to the War for Talent? Well, let's take a look at a field which is—to put it mildly—in a retention deficit. In 1998, the Society for Information Management did a survey of its members on recruitment and retention. They found that,

> "One of the main things IT professionals seek in an employer is a sense of community."
>
> Thomas Hoffman
> *Computerworld*[128]

Which ups the ante to not only buy pool tables for employees, but to also foster a climate of trust and fairness.

Corning Glass Works understood this dynamic, and ensured that their new recruits felt at home. They found that employees who participated in a formal, supportive orientation program were 69% more likely to remain with the company for three years than those who were left to flounder on their own.[129]

Pulling it all Together

Recently, Drs. Martin Shain and Jack Santa-Barbara elegantly summarized the research compendium on what drives superior health and safety results.[130] A composite of the Demand/Control, and the Effort/Reward dynamics, the *toxic work environment* is characterized by a workplace where employees have high *psychological demands* placed on them, and these are not balanced by a high degree of *control* over how work is done. Employees are also expending a high degree of *effort*, and do not feel they are receiving sufficient *reward* in return. In these workplaces, sickness and absenteeism cases rocket:

➢ *Back pain* and *heart problems* are 3x higher

➢ *Conflicts, mental health problems, injuries* and *infections* are 3x higher

➢ *Substance abuse* is 2x higher; and

➢ *Certain cancers* are 5x higher.

As Dr. Terrence Sullivan, President of the Institute for Work and Health notes of company management practices,

> *"This is where the gold is in my view, in terms of improving the health of the working population."*[131]

Stand by for Chapter 6, where I outline how these linkages can be captured in an enterprise Strategy Map.

Research Highlights: Employee Capability, Engagement, and Commitment

We've done a drive-by of the research on workplace drivers of health. Let's now turn our attention to the other half of the puzzle: the research compendium on employee capability, commitment, recruitment, and retention. The parallels are exciting!

The Cycle of Capability

> *"About two-thirds of employees' satisfaction levels were caused by just three factors:... latitude... authority... and knowledge and skills needed to serve customers. When combined with rewards for serving customers well, these factors in total accounted for over three-fourths of the job satisfaction experienced by these frontline workers..."*
>
> Heskett J.L., Sasser W.E., Schlesinger L.A.
> *The Service Profit Chain*

In the highly acclaimed research on the Service Profit Chain, Harvard researchers share the workplace research on the "*Cycle of Capability*"—the key drivers of employee ability to deliver results to customers.

The Cycle of Capability (Fig. 15) highlights the key drivers of capability: careful employee selection; high quality training and supports to do the job; latitude to meet customer needs, within the context of clearly defined expectations and constraints; and rewards and recognition aligned with good performance.

Citing research from an insurance company, Leonard Schlesinger and Jeffrey Zornitsky examined the key drivers of frontline employee capability.[132]

Listed in descending order of explanatory power, these include:

- ***Latitude*** to meet customer needs (36.6%)
- ***Authority*** to serve the customer (19.2%)
- ***Knowledge and skills*** to serve the customer (12.9%); and
- ***Rewards*** for serving customers well (7.3%).

Figure 15

The Cycle of...Capability *and* Health!

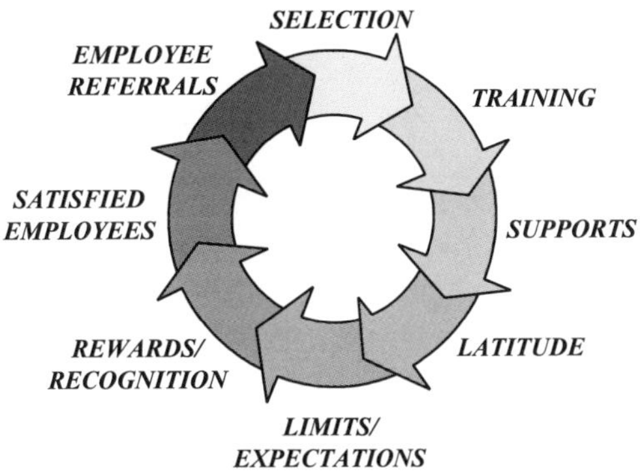
SELECTION
TRAINING
SUPPORTS
LATITUDE
LIMITS/
EXPECTATIONS
REWARDS/
RECOGNITION
SATISFIED
EMPLOYEES
EMPLOYEE
REFERRALS

Adapted from Heskett *et al., The Service Profit Chain*, 1997 with permission from the authors.

When I first read about the Cycle of Capability, I was captivated. What a powerful way to position health! This is the win/win I've been looking for.

The Cycle of Capability is a goldmine because it captures the two key engines of superior health outcomes: the Effort/Reward dynamic, and the Demand/Control dynamic.

In other words, I submit the Cycle of Capability is also the Cycle of Health!

Common Capability Drivers

> *"Employee capability simply suggests that when employees have both technical and social know-how, they are more able to accomplish work."*
>
> Ulrich D., Zenger J., Smallwood N.
> *Results-Based Leadership*[133]

In their forthcoming book entitled the *HR Scorecard: Linking People, Strategy, and Performance*, authors David Ulrich, Brian Becker and Mark Huselid outline the key elements of human resources transformation through a Human Resources (HR) Scorecard.[134] Preceding the publication of their book, Drs. Becker and Huselid shared their research insights on the "*Best and Worst HR Systems*" at a Balanced Scorecard Collaborative NetConference.[135] This research, based on four national surveys of over 2,800 firms, focused on the gaps between the bottom 10% of Human Resources Systems, and the top 10%.

What excites me about their findings is that many of the key elements of the Cycle of Capability (and Health) are reflected in this comparison between worst and best HR Systems. I share with you in Figure 16 a sneak preview of their findings, generously shared by these researchers, that I have translated into the health context:

Figure 16

Comparing the Best and Worst HR Systems[123]

COMPONENT OF CYCLE OF CAPABILITY/HEALTH	BOTTOM 10%	TOP 10%
Supports % with a formal grievance program % with a formal information sharing program Extent to which mission is clear	59% 47% 1.90	95% 96% 5.03
Rewards/Recognition % received performance appraisal %Performance appraisals based on objective measures	60% 13%	96% 63%

Source: Brian R. Becker and Mark A. Huselid, *Comparing the Best and Worst HR Systems*. Excerpted and adapted with permission from the authors.

Professor David Ulrich has done extensive work on the drivers of employee capability and commitment, both at the individual level, and the group level.[137] There are differences between how Ulrich, and Schlesinger of *Service Profit Chain* fame define capability and commitment, but they seem to agree on the importance of the following factors in driving up results.

These include:

- *Flexible* work arrangements.
- *Decision latitude*—Employees are given choice over which projects they work on, and how they execute them. This increases what Ulrich calls, "Work Impact".
- *Growth opportunities* – Ulrich's work addresses the esteem which comes from learning and applying new skills and knowledge.
- *Rewards* for a job well done.
- A sense of *community*.

Once again, social support—key driver of wellbeing—raises its head as a driver of commitment—and business results.

> "A worker's relationship with peers, supervisors and executives remains one of the biggest predictors of commitment."
>
> Ulrich D., Zenger J., Smallwood J.
> *Results-Based Leadership*[138]

The Gallup 12

> "Measuring the strength of a workplace can be simplified to twelve questions… (which) measure the core elements needed to attract, focus, and keep the most talented employees."
>
> Buckingham M., Coffman C.
> *First, Break all the Rules*[139]

The Gallup Organization has also been in search of the Holy Grail of performance drivers. After interviewing over a million employees, and 80,000 high performance managers, they arrived at the *"Twelve Statements for Employees"* (*The Q^{12} Advantage®*) — truisms which are correlated with at least one of the following business outcomes:

- *Productivity;*
- *Profit;*
- *Employee retention;*
- *Customer satisfaction;* and
- *Safety*

Gallup's definition of a healthy workplace is more general than literal (so far), but still forms a fascinating backdrop for our examination of health. These statements, presented in Chapter 6, address internal service/quality and leadership, most notably the caliber of the immediate manager.

In a not-so-subtle jibe at Hewitt and Associates' *"100 Best Companies to Work For"* survey, The Gallup Organization presents convincing evidence that the *100-Best* criteria miss the mark. I have to agree on this account. As Buckingham and Coffman note in their Gallup bestseller, *"First, Break all the Rules",*

> *"...if your relationship with your manager is fractured, then no amount of in-chair massaging or company-sponsored dog-walking will persuade you to stay and perform."*[140]

Employee Commitment and the Canada @ Work Study

> "...there is a direct link between management's
> acknowledgement of employees' personal lives,
> to the likelihood that they will stay with their employer,
> recommend their company as a good place to work,
> and promote its products and services."
>
> Royal Bank and Aon Consulting Inc.
> *Canada @ Work Study*™ [141]

In a 1999 national study, Aon Consulting partnered with the Royal Bank Financial Group to examine the drivers of employee commitment. The study hammered another nail in the coffin of pay as the arbiter of retention—suggesting that 62% of Canadians would jump ship if offered a raise of 20% or *less*. Once again, culture—not pay—is king, in retaining valued employees. In their cover page report on the study, MacLean's Magazine cited the top "Attitude Adjusters" as:

> "Management's recognition of the importance of an employee's *personal and family life*;
> Opportunities for *personal growth*;
> Belief that the *company satisfies customer* needs;
> Receiving *competitive pay*; and
> Belief that *coworkers are keeping pace* with the skills their jobs demand."

> "Overall... Canadians are committed to their employers
> and are willing to work hard, but will do so only if
> they feel the organization values them as much
> as it cares about customers and shareholders."[142]

Employee Recruitment and Retention Success

In 1998, Prudential Insurance conducted a similar study on what drives employee recruitment and retention success.[143] Prudential received a prestigious Catalyst award for their diversity initiatives, which are linked with management compensation. Once again, we see the familiar themes of leadership, internal service/quality, and work organization cropping up. According to this study, the top drivers of recruitment and retention success are:

- Open *communication*
- *Work/Life* balance
- *Management* quality
- *Supervisor* quality; and
- The nature of work.

Common Drivers of Sustainable High Performance

If we take a look at the drivers of *sustainable* high performance—as outlined by Canadian researchers such as Dr. Gordon Betcherman[144] we find that the common drivers include:

- *Meaningful involvement* and participation by employees in their work
- *Rewarding work*, with high psychic pay (intrinsic rewards)
- *Outstanding 360° communication*; and
- *Work/life balance*

Revisiting the bestseller, "*Built to Last*", Drs. Collins and Porras focus on the characteristics of enduring and Olympian corporate performance.[145] Their visionary companies are perhaps best characterized by the relentless pursuit of *alignment*. It would appear this pays off, since the visionary companies achieved cumulative stock returns outperforming the general market by a stunning factor of 15 between 1926 and 1990!

Key traits of these visionary companies include:

➤ Enduring core values

➤ A purpose that transcends profits

➤ An unslakable thirst for improvement, manifested in BHAGS, or Big Hairy Audacious Goals

➤ Employees passionate about the organization.

As Collins so eloquently states in a subsequent article,

> "...the essence of greatness does not lie in cost cutting, restructuring, or the pure profit motive. It lies in people's dedication to building companies around a sense of purpose—around core values that infuse work with the kind of meaning that goes beyond just making money."
>
> Collins J.
> Built to Flip. *Fast Company*[146]

CONNECTING THE DOTS

As my esteemed colleague Dr. Martin Shain once commented to me, "*This is a matter of joining the dots—in other words an exercise in logic, rather than empiricism.*"[147] Admittedly, I am only scratching the surface of two mammoth bodies of research, and there is ample room for researchers to put the fine strokes to this integrative work.

But the existing evidence is already enticing. We can produce extraordinary health *and* business results—if we do a good enough job in leadership and internal service/quality.

The important issue in my mind is not whether these linkages between health, capability, and high performance hold water, but rather how quickly you early adopters can take this ball and run with it!

LEADERSHIP CHECK-UP

The Capability/Wellbeing Synergy

1) Does your leadership team recognize the link between:
   a) Employee capability and wellbeing?
   b) Employee capability and financial results?

2) What are you currently *doing* to improve employee capability? [148]
   a) Do employees get the training they need to excel at their jobs?
   b) How well engineered are your support systems?
   c) How much latitude do your employees have to deliver results to customers?
   d) Have you clearly defined the limits within which frontline employees are enabled to act?
   e) How well and how frequently are employees recognized and rewarded for doing a good job?
   f) How objective are your employee performance measures?
   g) How tightly are employee rewards linked with objective customer satisfaction results?

3) Do you measure the impact of capability and leadership development initiatives on health and safety outcomes?

5

IF QUALITY CAN BE FREE, HEALTH CAN BE TOO!

*"**Health** is free, but no one is ever going to know it if there isn't some agreed-upon system of measurement"*

Adapted from, Crosby P.
Quality is Free

FOOTPRINTS FROM THE QUALITY JOURNEY

Some 30 years ago, leading organizations were captivated by news of a fantastical correlation between service/quality excellence and high performance. The PIMS data (*Profit Impact of Market Strategy*) from the Strategic Planning Institute in Cambridge, Massachusetts, revealed that organizations which had outstanding quality enjoyed unheard-of growth, and profitability *ten times better* than their mediocre counterparts![149]

The intrepid early adopters placed faith in this new wave of evidence—and began the journey toward service/quality excellence.[150]

Accounting for the Cost of Quality

Using methodology later known as Cost of Quality (COQ) accounting, they targeted Total Costs as their improvement target, and judiciously invested in Prevention activities, dramatically reducing the nefarious tail-end Failure Costs. The pioneers in quality also debunked the Law of Diminishing Returns (the myth that you can have "too much" quality), and aggressively pursued a goal of radical and continuous improvement. They blew their competition out of the water! In fact, nowadays the leaders are pursuing Six Sigma process quality, or quality at the level of ~ one defect in a million.

Finally, the leaders in quality took the maxim, "*You Get what You Measure*" to heart, and held their managers accountable not only for productivity and profits, but also quality. They then ensured that managers down the line had the tools, competencies, and incentive to improve quality. Quality was an issue which pervaded the organization, and it became everyone's job. It no longer sufficed to have someone at the end of the line to deal with the failures.

But the road to service/quality excellence has had its potholes. In fact one of the problems with the quality movement is that, while we've done an excellent job with *process* quality, many still miss the boat on *people-focused* quality.

Accounting for the Cost of Health

Managers have not *chosen* to ignore the business of employee wellbeing on productivity. They have simply not had the tools to measure it. So the vast majority of North American organizations unwittingly, but nonetheless strategically, invest in Failure Costs. Health is viewed as a fixed, if not constantly increasing cost.

Our emphasis is at the tail end of the horse! How can we justify a health investment strategy based on failure costs (illness care), and at the same time pursue Six-Sigma process quality?

From Silo Accounting to TOTAL Health Costs

> *"Safety, like quality, improves when we improve the system, not when we hire more specialists to find defects or remove hazards."*
>
> Deming W.E.
> *Minerva News*[151]

Arguments abound on the business case for a healthy workplace. Most of these fit into the category of creeping incrementalism. (*"If you do wellness program A, you'll get a 3:1 return on your investment"*). Not a great way to differentiate the value of health, from other competing improvement opportunities ("*If you fix Machine A, you'll get a 4:1 return on your investment.*")

> *How can we expect to capture the hearts of our leaders unless we WOW them with an **irresistible** business case?*

Sci-fi buffs will tell you that there is a world of difference between merely going "faster" in space, and moving up to "hyperspace". The film *2,001 A Space Odyssey* provides a vivid example of this quantum leap in speed.

Advocates for employee health must resist the urge to pepper leaders and investors with mind-numbing tales of cost containment minutiae. Instead, they must come to the plate with tangible evidence of how leaders can *supercharge* the human performance engine. And thanks to the Balanced Scorecard and Service Profit Chain, we can. (How do we do this? Stay tuned for Chapter 6)

The first step in this mission is to keep our focus on the big picture: **Total** Health Costs. This general model was eloquently described by Professors Randy Kudar and Angela Downey in *CMA Magazine*.[152]

The second step is to capture the elusive **Opportunity Costs** of stress, illness, and injury. Far too many organizations indulge a knee-jerk reaction against spending more on Good Costs (prevention, and up-front detection), because they don't recognize the impact of their investment on the Bad (direct and indirect failure costs) and Ugly failure costs (opportunity costs)![153]

> *"...corporations today are more likely to pursue cost containment as their paramount objective in negotiating with health plans and in structuring benefit packages with employees."*
>
> Robert Kuttner
> *The New England Journal of Medicine*[154]

But is this wise? This head-in-the-sand approach guarantees that failure costs will continue to thrive. We put an end to this accounting folly in the quality paradigm—it's time to also snuff out silo accounting for health. The Cost of Health model provides a simple rubric that you can use to evaluate your investment portfolio in Good, Bad, and Ugly employee health costs (Fig. 17).

Figure 17

The Organizational Health Investment Profile©

Where are you spending your health dollars?

THE GOOD		THE BAD		THE UGLY
Prevention Costs	Detection Costs	Failure Costs		
		Direct Costs	Indirect Costs	Opportunity Costs
__$	__$	__$	__$	__$

Copyright Healthy Business Inc., 2000.

We need to apply Cost of Health analysis in two key areas:

➤ *To high-quality management* of each individual health care issue (after the fact); and

➤ *To effective prevention*, before illness and injury occur.

The Total Cost of Disease and Disability

There is abundant evidence that high-quality health care education and management dramatically reduce the *severity and frequency* of diseases… and that this is good for the bottom line. We just need to see the forest, as well as the trees.

Example: The Total Cost of Asthma

Let's take a look at a hot medical issue, and use the province of Alberta as our petri dish.

Asthma is consistently rated as one of the top five health issues—by cost and prevalence—for Alberta employers. At the City of Calgary, this is no exception. But our traditional accounting systems have eroded our ability to treat asthma, because they focus on the escalation in prevention costs, not our ability to dramatically reduce failure costs.

Firstly, let's understand that asthma is the kind of condition which severely disrupts workplace productivity. Whether it's an employee with asthma or a dependent, an asthma attack in your family can railroad your work plans for several days. And simmering asthma problems can also significantly affect productivity. The Calgary Asthma Program, for example, has found a link between the moderately to severe asthmatic, and sleep deprivation and depression. [156] Which makes the turnaround results by the Community Asthma Care Clinics—a 70 – 90% reduction of night terrors—all the more significant.[157]

Let me give you an optic for the Total Cost of Asthma—when it is well managed. In a compelling asthma study reported in *Managed Healthcare*, the following Total Health Cost profile emerged:[158]

How to slash your Total Costs of Asthma by 30%

- *Invest substantially in anti-inflammatory medications.* There are two types of medications which asthma patients take. One is a preventive type of medication, which reduces the inflammation of the airways. The other (typically *Ventolin*) is meant for treatment of breakthrough symptoms. So the anti-inflammatory medications represent a prevention cost.

- *Invest in a 6% increase in planned absenteeism* for employees to attend asthma clinics.

- *Measure the impact on your failure costs.* Effective asthma management reduces days hospitalized by 77%, asthma-related emergency visits by 48%, and urgent care visits by 32%. This affects workplace productivity whether your health costs are publicly or privately insured.

- This is where the rubber hits the road. *Sum up your prevention, detection and failure buckets*, to arrive at a net 30% reduction in Total Asthma Costs.

Figure 18

Turnaround in Total Asthma Costs

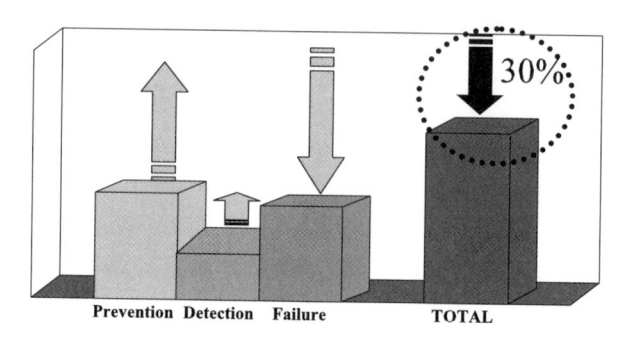

Prevention   Detection   Failure   TOTAL

30%

Note that this argument dramatically understates the benefits of asthma care because it once again omits the *opportunity costs* of lost productivity, creativity, and quality among affected employees and their co-workers.

Bucking the Trend toward Cost Containment

Organizations such as Motorola in the U.S. have intuitively taken the step toward proactive care, by determining that their core values of *quality* and *people focus* should drive their health investment decisions, not cost containment. Massive layoffs notwithstanding, Motorola has demonstrated that significant cost savings and human benefits both accrue from such an enlightened strategic health focus. In doing so, Motorola has moved away from the knee-jerk cost-containment approach to health cost inflation, which inevitably increases total health costs.[159]

As another example of this investment approach to employee health, the Ontario government provides free 'flu shots to all residents, with a solid understanding that the savings far outweigh the up-front costs.[160]

The Total Cost of Disease/Disability Prevention

Cost of Health analysis can also be applied to our Prevention strategy—and this gives us another exciting spin on our accounting. Now don't change that channel while I explain how accounting can be exciting.

I've shared with you in Chapter 4 that enlightened leadership practices can easily chop stress, illness, and injury rates in *half*. And we now know that these same leadership practices are called for in the normal pursuit of business excellence.

So when we apply our new understanding of what really drives workplace stress, illness, and injury, not only can health be free, but a big chunk of our prevention bucket turns out to be free!

Figure 19

If Quality can be Free, Health can be Too!

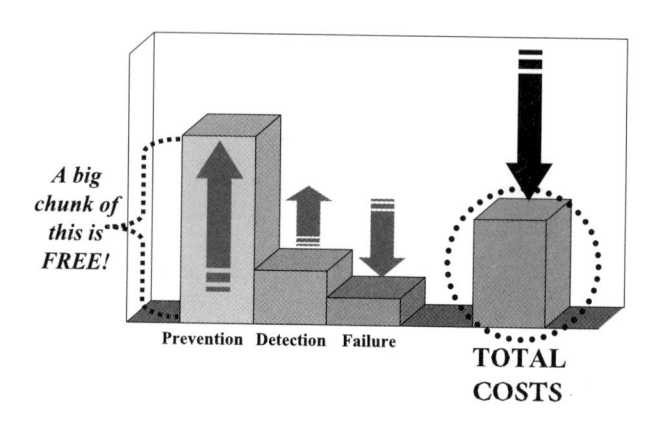

A big chunk of this is FREE!

Prevention Detection Failure   **TOTAL COSTS**

The reality is that many organizations already have budgets allocated for leadership development. Most organizations also have non-strategic initiatives from which resources could be readily diverted. As Dr. Kaplan has noted, winners in Balanced Scorecard implementation achieve turnaround results by using *existing* resources within their organizations. The dollars are already there—they just need to be redeployed strategically.[161] The acid test, of course, is whether leaders are being held accountable for people results.

In their forthcoming book on the HR Scorecard, authors Ulrich, Becker, and Huselid address our dual mandate for *cost containment* as well as *value creation*.[162] Cultural improvement represents a beautiful example of how we can indeed profit while reducing pain.

As Ted Pattenden, CEO of NRI Inc. commented on his dramatic reduction of injury event and severity rates from 3800 lost days in 1990 to 16 in 1999[163]:

> *"This was not an issue of throwing money at (health and safety), this was an issue of throwing management intensity at it."* [164]

In fact, during the period in which National Rubber slashed lost time injuries by ten, and lost time days by 25, their net profits increased from −12.2% to +5.1%.[165]

> *"...safety and business performance can go hand in hand as the concurrent results of the application of the same management principles and practices... those organizations that have learned how to be multi-ball jugglers, that can deliver excellence in safety along with productivity, quality and the other factors that lead to superior profits, will have an enduring competitive advantage."*
>
> Dr. Jim Stewart
> *Business Quarterly*[166]

Strategic Health Focus: Reducing Exposure to Health Cost Inflation

Another benefit emerges from reducing event rates and costs per event, and this is the reduction in exposure to health cost inflation. Let's think of this as three levels of exposure (Fig. 20).

The "Do Nothing" Scenario. We know that the "Do-nothing" scenario is a chilling alternative, both because of the graying of the workforce, and the abundance of new medical technologies. Pitney Bowes Inc. received a rude awakening in the 1990's when they examined what health cost inflation would do to their profits if they didn't intervene in the next decade:

> *"An analysis of health care expenditures in 1991 revealed that escalation of health care costs would eclipse growth in corporate profits by the year 2000."*
>
> C. Everett Koop
> National Health Award Winners[167]

This account underscores the peril of standing still in organizational health strategy: things are only going to get worse. This scenario, represented in the top line of Figure 20, is what many organizations are already seeing in their rear-view mirror.

Health "Management". The middle line in Figure 20 represents the impact which health management can have on health cost inflation. We have seen how many organizations are now managing disease and disability with stunning results. In many cases, this involves simple, but timely interventions which dramatically improve health and productivity outcomes.

Corporate Health Consultants, for example achieve an across-the-board 30% reduction in disability rates when they provide mediation between employee and employer needs in return-to-work.[168]

But regrettably, it is also in vogue to "manage" health—or should I say, to manage health costs—simply by limiting insurance coverage. In a 1998 survey by Applied Management Consultants, more than 20% of Canadian drug plans for major employers had already implemented coverage ceilings, mandatory (generic drug) substitution, restrictive drug formularies, and cost-shifting from the employer to the employee. Interestingly, employee wellness programs were being considered by more than 50% of these drug plans, to help control costs.[169]

While cost shifting to the employee admittedly reduces employer coverage to direct health costs, it does nothing to limit employer exposure to the indirect and opportunity costs.

Either way, however, the "*Managing Health*" option is less costly in the short-term than standing still.

Preventing Event Rates and Managing Health. But the most spectacular benefit arises for organizations which slash event rates, *and* costs per event. This is a *multiplier* effect, and organizations which go this route enjoy a stunning buffer from health cost inflation.

For example,

... when NRI reduced their injury rate by a factor of 10, and their severity rate (days lost) by a factor of 25, they reduced their health cost exposure by a factor of 250!

112   Chapter 5   If Quality can be Free, Health can be Too!

This is reflected in the steep downturn in health costs in the lowest bar of Figure 20.

Figure 20

Reduce Event Rate and Cost/Event to Reduce Exposure to Health Cost Inflation

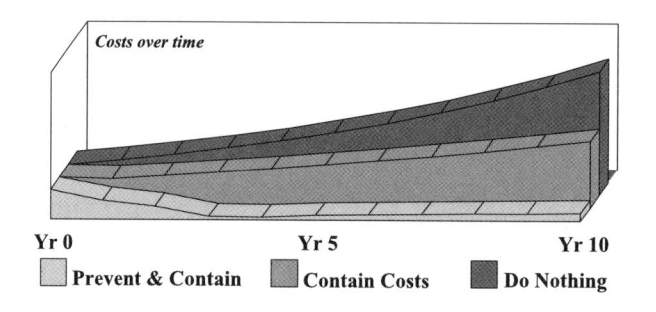

Costs over time

Yr 0　　　　　　　Yr 5　　　　　　　Yr 10

☐ Prevent & Contain　　■ Contain Costs　　■ Do Nothing

Why Silo Accounting Hurts Us

When we account for health, we typically place costs for benefits, medications, and Worker's Compensation premiums as line items in a statement of expense. This type of silo accounting hurts us. And here's why:

1) *Silo accounting creates alarm out of context.* When we assess variances from year to year, we can't help be appalled by double-digit health cost inflation. Two potent drivers for this include population aging (Fig. 21), and the availability of, and appetite for new medical technologies.

Figure 21

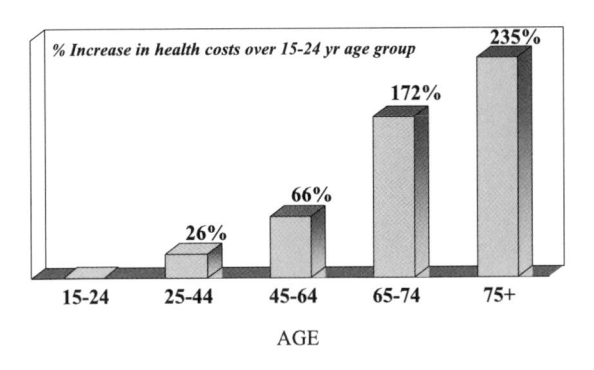

How Aging Affects Health Costs

% Increase in health costs over 15-24 yr age group

- 15-24:
- 25-44: 26%
- 45-64: 66%
- 65-74: 172%
- 75+: 235%

AGE

Source: Alberta Health Statistics, 1997.

But our population is going to age whether we like it or not. More meaningful is information on whether we are winning the war against stress, illness, and injury. Are we reducing event rates? Are we improving disease, disability, and rehabilitation outcomes? Are we reducing opportunity costs? In other words, are we reducing the Burden of Illness?

And is our appetite for medical advancements a bad thing? The medical research community is continually being exhorted to speed toward medical cures. And the advancement of medical research is taken by many in this field as a very serious responsibility. So when medical pioneers such as the University of Calgary's Dr. Ji-Won Yoon announce that they have arrived at a cure for diabetes in lab rats, the potential benefits for the health system—much less the personal benefits to people with diabetes—are staggering.[170] No wonder our ears perk up.

2) *Silo accounting creates complacency without cause.*

When health costs go down, many leaders mistakenly assume that they have won the health war. In fact the reverse can be true.

For example, managed care in the U.S. has reduced health cost inflation dramatically (if you're measuring silo costs) but primarily through cost shifting from employers to employees. Total costs tell another picture: health outcomes have in fact deteriorated, and real costs have increased.[171]

Similarly, reference-based pricing in British Columbia has decreased direct provincial drug costs, but has increased overall health costs.[172] It appears this has just been an exercise in squeezing the balloon.

3) *Silo accounting does not capture cause and effect.* Most importantly, our traditional accounting for health commits the cardinal sin in strategy management: it does not capture cause and effect. And this snuffs out our ability to validate our investments in health and human capital.

Sneak Preview: Cost of Health and the Balanced Scorecard

If the Balanced Scorecard is all about cause and effect, then we need a better way to account for health. Just as we did in the quality movement, we need to target the high-impact areas for employee health improvements.

How might we do this? In my work with the City of Calgary, we are targeting Total Health Costs in our pilot scorecard. And we're only biting off as much as we can chew.

We recognize that many quality initiatives were deep-sixed by quality gladiators, throwing all available resources at any conceivable quality improvement project. While this is a very effective way to drain the coffers, it is a sure road to failure.

We've begun by identifying the *top five* health issues for the organization by prevalence and cost.[173] We do this by analyzing aggregate data from insurance benefits, drug claims and dollars to identify the top health issues—by financial and human impact—for the organization. Like peeling an onion, we can then target our interventions, our accounting, and our limited resources to high impact issues.

There are several ways we can arrive at this Top Five list. On the one hand, it is helpful to order these by direct cost impact. Admittedly this has clout with executive teams—at least in the short term. But I prefer to lean toward prevalence and severity as my guide, since this ultimately translates into substantial indirect and opportunity costs—that underside of the health cost iceberg. And I like to achieve a balance between "quick hits", and long-term strategic improvements.

With the assistance of Health Canada's *Workplace Health Survey*, and Glaxo Wellcome's *Health Evidence*™ process, we've narrowed down the City of Calgary's top five health issues (by claim) to:

1) Respiratory

2) Cardiovascular

3) Mental disorders

4) Musculoskeletal disorders; and

5) Digestive disorders.[174]

We then roll the Top 5 into a Total Cost of Health Index, and embed this within the corporate scorecard. If the index goes up, we are losing the battle to reduce health costs. If the index goes down, we are proving our ability to reduce total health costs. And we know we can bring that index down!

As time progresses, we will conquer some health issues, and add others to the Index. Our accounting approach enables us to be active and successful participants, rather than passive bystanders to health cost inflation. Most importantly, it will educate the City of Calgary's executive team—quarter after quarter—on the strategic value of employee health.

The Institute for Health and Productivity Management (IHPM) has embarked on a similar mission to identify key health issues based on aggregate employer results. IHPM divided disease categories into the top five most expensive physical, and mental conditions. Not surprisingly, cardiovascular, gastrointestinal, and mental disorders—such as depressive episodes—figure prominently on these lists.[175]

THE COST OF OPTING OUT

Be careful what you wish for...
you might just get it.

We are witnessing a significant, but misguided trend in North America as corporations pull back from their direct investment in employee and family health. Like rats jumping from a sinking ship, workplaces are casting away their financial ties with employee wellbeing, and offering financial inducements for employees and their families to go it alone. It is assumed that it's too messy and expensive for workplaces to be in the health benefits business.

> *"The "take-up" rate—that is, the proportion of workers who actually got (health) insurance— fell from 88.3 percent in 1987 to 80.1 percent in 1996.*
>
> *... employees with families generally exhaust the cash value of their employer-provided benefits, and must either tap their salary income to pay the additional costs of family coverage, or do without."*
>
> Robert Kuttner
> *New England Journal of Medicine*[176]

We are witnessing the same cost shift from employers to employees in Canada in our extended health benefits: our flexible benefit plans and our spending accounts.

But it's a little academic to worry about getting your hands dirty when you're waist-deep in mud. If workplaces were to measure their Total Cost of Health, they would receive a rude awakening.

By giving up control over investments in employee health, workplaces have lost their ability to staunch the bleeding in their opportunity costs.

They have lost a powerful lever for cost-effective health decisions. And—like it or not—they continue to invest in the indirect and opportunity costs of health.

For example, workplaces that opt out of benefit coverage can no longer support employees to take costly migraine medications. Cash-strapped employees will simply elect to take the time off work.

The same workplaces can no longer provide the best in asthma care, so employees with dependents with asthma would be absent less often. And they can no longer use drug analysis data to identify the top productivity hits for the organization.

> *Now it's all up to the employee.*
> *And if employees don't want (or can't afford)*
> *to get optimal care, they won't.*

Carpe diem in Health Management

When it comes to rehabilitating ill or injured employees, timing is everything. In fact there is a burning platform for action, because as time passes, so do an employee's chances of *ever* returning to work.

> *It is commonly accepted that if an employee is*
> *away on short-term disability for 6 months,*
> *their chances of **ever** returning to work are 50%.*

This drops to 10% at one year, and 5% at two years, resulting in staggering long-term disability, employee, and social costs.[177]

The onus is on workplaces—at least the ones who are tuned in to the retention crisis—to get employees back to work as soon as possible. But for workplaces who have pulled out of health coverage, or drastically scaled back their involvement, they leave it to the whims of providers. And there is always the danger that providers—earning a premium on every treatment they provide—will not be as motivated to reduce event and severity rates.

Afterthought

Many years ago I had the opportunity to stay at a research station on Heron Island, a veritable jewel on the Great Barrier Reef. One of the researchers shared stories about his fascinating work with tiger sharks. He would head out in his boat each day to feed them scraps of fish, and observe their behavior. And he cheerfully noted, *"I'm almost at the point where I can get in the water with them."*

I still wonder what happened when he did.

The message for workplaces is there: when you give away the power, it can hurt.

LEADERSHIP CHECK-UP

From Quality Focus to Health Focus

1) How much emphasis do your leaders place on quality improvement?

2) What does your investment profile for *process quality* look like for:
   a) *Prevention*
   b) *Detection*
   c) *Failure costs?*

3) How do you currently account for health?
   a) *Silo Accounting;* or
   b) *Total Cost of Health?*

4) What does your investment profile for *health* look like for:
   a) *Prevention*
   b) *Detection*
   c) *Failure costs?*

5) Do you exercise positive influence over employee wellbeing… or have you opted out?

Section II

THE HEALTHY SCORECARD

*Good health
is good leadership
is great business...*

and we can prove it!

6

LINKING HEALTH INTO THE BALANCED SCORECARD

You've got to think about "big things" while doing small things, so that all the small things go in the right direction.

Alvin Toffler

UNTAPPED EXCELLENCE: THE SEARS MODEL

So far I have waxed poetic on what is largely correlative data that good health is good leadership. Now for the *pièce de résistance*—the **causal** data that, "*Good health is good leadership is great business*".

"*We are confronted with insurmountable opportunities.*"

Pogo

Recently a number of stellar organizations have unwittingly uncovered a breathtaking business case for healthy leadership. In 1998 I stumbled across an article which revolutionized the way I approach health strategy and performance measurement. In the January/February 1998 issue of *Harvard Business Review*, authors Rucci, Kirn, and Quinn wrote on *The Employee-Customer-Profit Chain at Sears*.[178]

Now Sears had a 70-point employee survey. Through a statistical process called causal pathway modeling, the Sears management team distilled this survey down to a ten-point index: the employee drivers, which they found to have a ***causal*** relationship with customer, and financial results.

*Sears not only found a correlation between employee satisfaction, customer loyalty, and the bottom line, they found a **causal** link!*

Every time the ten-point employee index increased by 5%, the Sears management team could *predict* that, 3 months down the road, customer loyalty—as measured by repeat purchases, share of wallet, depth of relationship, *et cetera*—would increase by 1.3%. And they could *predict* that 3 months hence, revenues would increase by 0.5%. This model, illustrated in Figure 22, was tested quarter after quarter, with stunning reliability. Quarter after quarter, managers saw this employee-customer-profit relationship play out.

Now for the result which knocked my socks off:

In 1997, as a result of improving employee satisfaction results by 4%, Sears predicted—and realized—an incremental $200 Million in revenues, and over a quarter of a billion dollars in market capitalization!

This is the kind of data that has executives and investors leaning forward in their seats!

Now this doesn't mean that organizations should rely on people results alone. After all, IBM delivered stellar employee results in the 1980's, yet almost committed strategic *hari kari* when it pursued mainframes instead of PC's.[179]

Figure 22

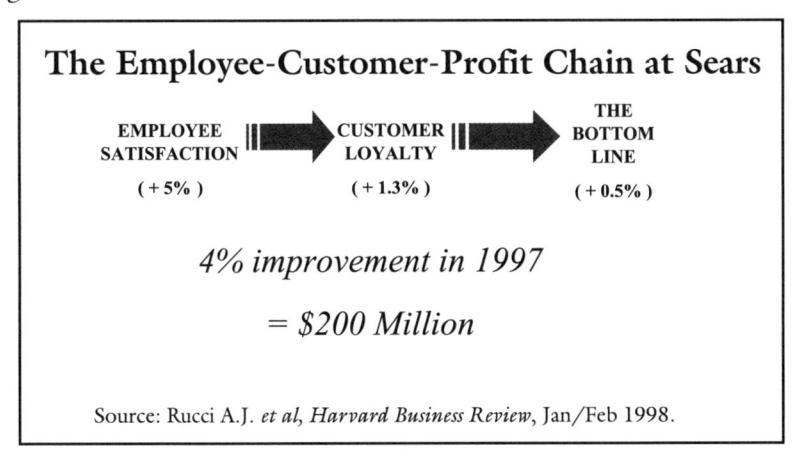

The Employee-Customer-Profit Chain at Sears

EMPLOYEE SATISFACTION (+5%) ▶ CUSTOMER LOYALTY (+1.3%) ▶ THE BOTTOM LINE (+0.5%)

4% improvement in 1997

= $200 Million

Source: Rucci A.J. *et al, Harvard Business Review*, Jan/Feb 1998.

> *What the Sears model teaches us is that we can <u>empirically</u> connect employee, customer, and financial results.*

What a compelling way to focus management attention on the drivers of the business! The Sears management team was deeply involved in developing this econometric model, and as a result bought into the radical—or is it intuitive?—notion to reward managers based on 1/3 employee satisfaction leading indicators, 1/3 customer loyalty leading indicators, and 1/3 trailing financial indicators.

Talk about putting your money where your mouth is! In translating the "softer side of Sears" into bottom-line outcomes, these leaders created a model that is intuitive, robust, and appealing for employees, managers, and investors alike.

<u>A deeper meaning to the Sears Service Profit Chain</u>

But I read the Sears story with health strategy in mind. And I was stunned by what I found. Hidden unwittingly in the Sears Index is a Health Index!

> *When you look at the Sears 10-point index, it reads inadvertently like a primer on the drivers of workplace health.*

Let's refresh your memory from Chapter 4 with a review of what sets the healthiest organizations apart from their mediocre counterparts[180]:

Figure 23

Key Components of a Healthy Culture [181]

- A sense of belonging and meaning
- Meaningful involvement
- Learning and challenge
- Social and supervisory support
- Job clarity
- Pride in workmanship
- Balance between job demands, and employee control over how work is performed
- Balance between effort and reward
- Physical working conditions
- Overall job satisfaction

Now let's look at key elements of the Sears 10-point index:

Figure 24

Could the Sears Index also be a Health Index?

KEY HEALTH DRIVERS	THE SEARS INDEX
A sense of belonging & meaning	➤ I *understand* our business strategy ➤ Do you *see a connection* between the work you do and the company's overall strategic objectives? ➤ *I am proud* to say I work at Sears
Social & supervisory support	➤ How does **the way you are treated** by those who supervise you influence your overall attitude about your job?
Balance between demands/control	➤ How does the **amount of work** you are expected to do influence your overall attutude about your job?
Balance between effort/reward	➤ My work gives me **a sense of accomplishment**
Physical working conditions	➤ How do your **physical working conditions** influence your overall attutude about your job?
Overall job satisfaction	➤ *I like the kind of work I do* ➤ *I feel good* about the future of the company. ➤ Sears is **making the changes necessary** to compete effectively.

Source for Sears Index: Rucci A.J., Kirn, S.P., Quinn, R.T. *Op. Cit.*

Could the Sears Index also be a Health Index?

You bet!

Sears has the bricks to link their Employee-Customer-Profit model with health outcomes and costs. But it needs the mortar to link the two.

Stand by for the Healthy Profit Chain© (Fig. 31), which illustrates how to make this link!

OTHER UNTAPPED HEALTH INDICES

A deeper meaning to the Gallup Top 12

Need more convincing? Let's take a look at the Gallup top-12 indicators: The Q^{12} *Advantage*®. Recall from Chapter 4 that the *Gallup 12* is definitively linked with superior business outcomes: productivity, profit, employee retention, customer satisfaction and safety.

Here's an illustration of why the Q^{12} *Advantage*® has clout. In 1997 Gallup was invited to examine a phenomenally successful retailer. They found that the stores with top quartile results on the 12-point survey outperformed bottom-quartile stores by *$104 Million* in sales per year. Top quartile stores exceeded profit targets by 14%, while bottom-quartile stores missed targets by 30%![183]

Figure 25

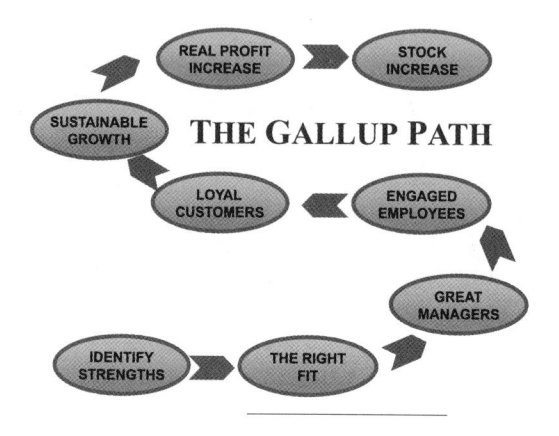

THE GALLUP PATH

Real Profit Increase → Stock Increase
Sustainable Growth
Loyal Customers ← Engaged Employees
Great Managers
Identify Strengths → The Right Fit

Source: The Gallup Path, www.gallup.com/path
Reprinted with permission The Gallup Organization Inc.
The Gallup Path is Copyright © 1977 The Gallup Organization

Based on this research, The Gallup Organization has defined a "Gallup Path", Copyright© 1997, The Gallup Organization, reprinted in Figure 25, to superior and sustained business outcomes.[184]

As you can see, "Great Managers" figure prominently in the path. But while The Gallup Organization speaks of healthier organizations, they, like Sears Roebuck, have not *explicitly* correlated their outstanding work with measured health outcomes. At least not yet.

Figure 26

Could the *Q^{12} Advantage*® also be a Health Index?

Key Health Drivers	The *Q^{12} Advantage* ®
A sense of belonging & meaning	1) The **purpose of my company** makes me feel my job is important.
Meaningful involvement	2) At work, **my opinions seem to count.**
Social and supervisory support	3) I have the **materials and equipment** I need to do my job right. 4) My supervisor, or the person I report to, seems to **care about me** as a person. 5) There is someone at work who **encourages my development.** 6) I have **a best friend** at work.
Job Clarity	7) **I know what is expected** of me.
Pride in workmanship	8) My associates (fellow employees) are **committed to doing quality work.**
Learning & challenge	9) This last year, I have had **opportunities to learn and grow.** 10) At work, I have the **opportunity to do what I do best** every day.
Balance between effort/reward	11) In the last seven days, I have received **praise for good work.** 12) In the last six months, someone at work has **talked to me about my progress.**

Source for the *The Q^{12} Advantage*®: Buckingham M., Coffman C., *Op.cit.*

*Like the Sears model,
the Gallup Path is begging
to have employee health
explicitly plugged into the equation.*

*The connection with health is inadvertent,
so these outstanding organizations
are still missing out on this
next quantum leap in
human capital and
business performance.*

Specifically, we need to capture event and severity rates for stress, illness, and injury, as well as Total Costs, which affect sustainable growth. Now all we need to do is reapply capability surveys to capture not only the leadership/profit link, but also the leadership/health link. And while organizations such as Gallup have not yet released the data to support this additional pathway toward sustainable growth, I believe the opportunity to expand their excellent work into a new frontier is profound. Explicitly building health into such models unveils the *full* path to sustainable growth.

Figure 27

The Missing Link

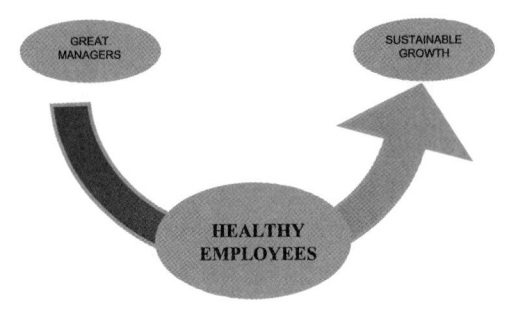

```
GREAT MANAGERS → HEALTHY EMPLOYEES → SUSTAINABLE GROWTH
```

Cheap, easy, and profitable! That is, if you really are serious about putting the quality of your managers in your value-creation equation.

The U.S. Department of Transportation, Procurement Measures

Let's take a look at another "sleeper" Capability/Wellbeing Index. The U.S. Department of Transportation (DOT) uses an electronic Balanced Scorecard survey for their Procurement officers.[185] This concise 12-point index captures employee attitudes on a quarterly basis. Thanks to a streamlined process (it takes only 5 minutes to complete the online survey), and commitment to action on survey findings, the DOT enjoys a spectacular 90% return rate for their employee surveys.[186] The DOT questions also read like a health survey: (Fig. 28)

Figure 28

Untapped Capability and Wellbeing Crossovers

KEY HEALTH DRIVERS	DEPARTMENT OF TRANSPORTATION MEASURES
Meaningful involvement	1) *Management seeks my opinions and ideas on important matters.*
Social and supervisory support	2) *I am provided with adequate tools to get my job done.*
Job Clarity	3) *(My colleagues) are well trained and understand their roles and responsibilities.*
Learning & challenge	4) *I receive adequate training to do my job.*
Pride in workmanship	5) *Management emphasises quality in our work products.* 6) *My services provide a cost benefit to our customer's program.*
Balance between effort/reward	7) *Contributions are recognized.*
Balance between demands/control	8) *I am given the authority to make appropriate decisions.*
Work/life balance	9) *My organization provides flexibility in my work schedule.*
Overall fairness	10) *Management properly balances the needs of the program office with the need to spend Federal funds wisely.* 11) *Operations are conducted in an ethical manner.*
Overall satisfaction	12) *Overall, how would you rate the quality of worklife?*

Source: U.S. Department of Transportation, Procurement Survey *Acquisition Balanced Scorecard Demo Data Collection Page:* Employee Demo Survey www.pie.dot.gov .

The Employee Capability/Wellbeing Index©

> *"How do you determine the key factors that affect employee well-being, satisfaction, and motivation?"*
>
> Malcolm Baldridge National Quality Program
> *Criteria for Performance Excellence 2001*[187]

For years I've been looking for a way to connect health with business strategy. Now we can draw from the mother lode of research on what drives capability, sustained high performance, and employee wellbeing, to arrive at a shortlist akin to a Maslow's Hierarchy of Needs:[188] an Employee Capability/Wellbeing Index©. And this index, together with the Cost of Health model, forms the heart of the Healthy Scorecard.

But how do we apply it? What about the Healthy Scorecard *process*?

Putting the Capability/Wellbeing Index© to Work

> *"Organizations that have constructed elaborate measurements and methods often find that the cost of maintaining them and difficulty of understanding them defeat their usefulness and guarantee that they will fall into disuse... those measures and methods we have found most useful have been designed to be simple, consistent, timely, and fair."*
>
> James L. Heskett, W. Earl Sasser, Leonard A. Schlesinger
> *The Service Profit Chain*[189]

The Employee Capability/Wellbeing Index is more a process than a finite list of measures. It enables us to have a credible starting point in our measurement of health and human capital—without taking months and years of lead-time to arrive at measures that already make sense.

Admittedly the concept of a Capability/Wellbeing Index represents heresy in the consulting world. What I am suggesting is that we DO start with a one-size-fits-all approach. I have yet to be convinced that there is a more effective way for leaders new to this health paradigm to short-cut their learning curve on what drives employee capability, wellbeing, and sustained high performance. Further, with the excellent trailblazing done by organizations such as Sears, Gallup, and the National Institute of Occupational Safety and Health, do we really need to reinvent the wheel?

Keys to Success

There are three prerequisites for an effective Employee Capability/Wellbeing Index. It must:

1) **Capture key drivers** of employee wellbeing *and* capability;
2) **Be predictively linked** with health, as well as customer and financial outcomes; and
3) **Be flexible** to reflect emerging priorities.

Prerequisite #1

*Capture key drivers of employee wellbeing **and** capability.*

As you can see, the Sears Index, The Gallup Organization's Q^{12} *Advantage*®, and the U.S. Department of Transportation Procurement survey already (albeit inadvertently) marry wellbeing and capability drivers. So if you lack the resources, critical mass, or time to conduct causal pathway modeling on your business drivers, don't be shy to benchmark.

*But having a powerful employee index
and not linking it with health outcomes
is a little like driving a Maserati
in a traffic jam.*

And this leads us to the next prerequisite…

<u>Prerequisite #2</u>

The Capability/Wellbeing Index must be predictively linked within a Balanced Scorecard or Employee-Customer-Profit Chain.

This is where we separate the men from the boys. For us to capture the true power of enlightened leadership, or great managers, the Employee Capability/Wellbeing Index must also be plugged *explicitly* into employee health outcomes and costs. And virtually no one is doing this yet on the corporate scorecard!

*There is a gaping chasm
—and stunning opportunity—
in the application of employee indices
to predict health and financial outcomes.*

The new reality is that we can lead for health *and* high performance. And the payoff for organizations pursuing enlightened leadership is even greater than first conceived.

Keep in mind that net after tax profits in the U.S. are exceeded by corporate health costs. And these corporate health costs ring in at over a trillion dollars![190]
Yet the foregoing research tells us we can readily chop health costs in half— simply by leading people and managing organizations better.

So how do we link wellbeing with the Balanced Scorecard? Very simply. As author Jim Clemmer would say, *"This isn't rocket surgery."* My client work centers on building a 10-15 point Employee Capability/Wellbeing Index, and linking this with critical Human Resource, Process, Customer, and Financial outcomes on the *corporate* scorecard. Clearly these measures will ultimately link with the strategic measures of a Human Resources Scorecard, or the higher resolution metrics of a *"Healthy Workplace"* Balanced Scorecard.[191] But—first and foremost—I want to ensure that the basic drivers of wellbeing and capability are prominent on the *corporate* radar screen.

Perhaps more importantly, I advocate including not only *outcome* indicators in the Learning & Growth perspective, but also leading indictors (such as the Capability/Wellbeing Index). This does go against standard BSC practice to focus on outcome measures. But I believe this departure is vital for us to really tell the story of human captial *cause-and-effect* in our Enterprise Strategy Maps.

The Healthy Scorecard provides an essential tool for us to educate leaders on what really drives people, and how this can supercharge strategic execution.

These are the kind of metrics that employees, external customers, and shareholders can enthusiastically buy into. They simply make sense.

Connecting the Dots: The Healthy Strategy Map

In *Harvard Business Review*, and in their latest tome, *The Strategy-Focused Organization*, Drs. Norton and Kaplan convey the value of a Strategy Map, a cause-and-effect optic for how human capital and other intangible assets are linked with process, customer and financial results.[192]

Let's take a look at the Strategy Map for building employee capability and wellbeing into the Balanced Scorecard: *The Healthy Strategy Map*©. (Fig. 29). This figure is key to understanding the Healthy Scorecard, so take your time to explore the predictive linkages.

1) **The central logic** is that the Capability/Wellbeing Index is a bellwether for the quality of work life, and leadership. This is not a stand-alone metric for the Learning and Growth perspective. Rather, it should also be supported by tightly focused strategic metrics for information systems, culture, and competencies.

2) ***When the Capability/Wellbeing Index improves***, organizations can expect improvements in their HR Outcomes Index, such as employee turnover, absenteeism, grievances, and illness rates, as well as improvements in customer results.

It is no coincidence when I find a client's business unit which rates poorly on leadership, and which also has high absenteeism and health care utilization, and poor customer results.

3) ***When critical business processes improve*** (including HR and health/safety processes), we can also expect improvements in HR Outcomes. For example, when GE instituted their *"Dumb Rules and Forms Committee"* to stamp out bureaucracy, employee satisfaction improved dramatically.[193] Tony Blair also had stakeholder satisfaction in mind when he announced a *"Bureaucracy Buster"* to tackle the National Health Service's red tape mountain.[194] Improving Internal Processes reduces the hassle factor for employees, and improves the quality of the work environment. Employees react by giving higher ratings on the Capability/Wellbeing Index.

4) ***When the HR Outcome Index improves***, so do financial results. There are two pathways for this improvement:

a) *Traditional direct costs are reduced*, such as Worker's compensation, drug costs, short and long-term disability costs. In addition indirect costs can be tracked, such as the cost to hire replacement labour, or the cost of equipment damage from an accident. We know these will go down when event rates are contained.

b) *Opportunity costs are also reduced*. Like a canary in a coalmine, when the Capability/Wellbeing Index deteriorates, we know there will be a trickle down effect—or a flood—to business results. And this is where the undiscovered value of health lies.

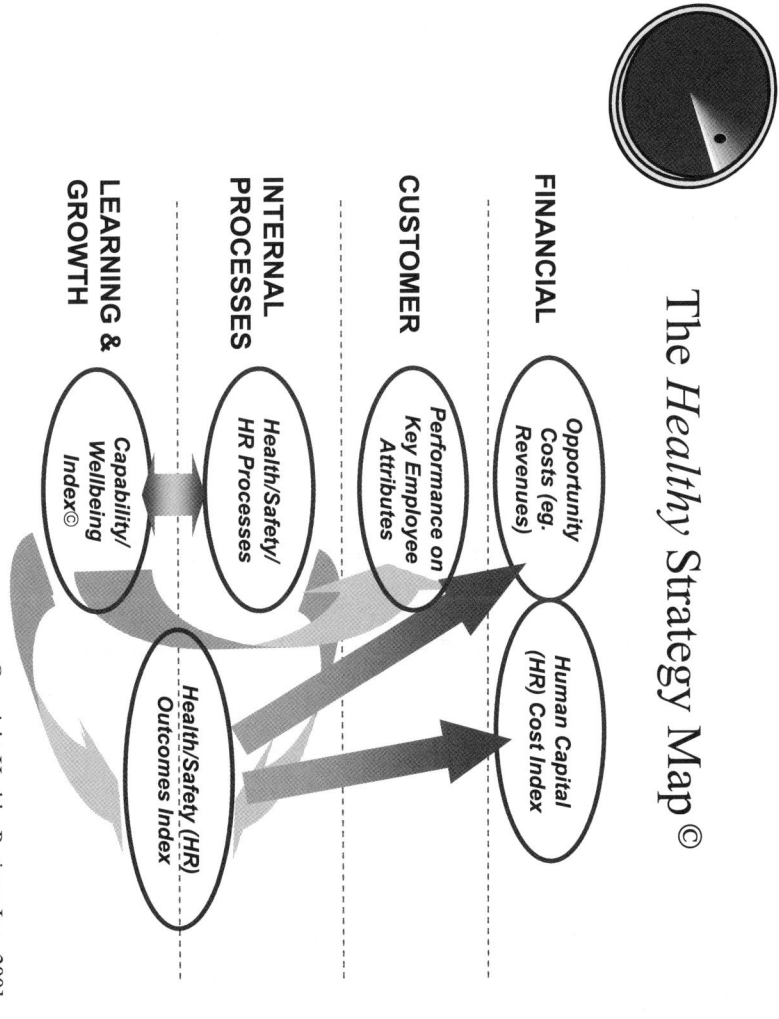

The Healthy Scorecard 143

Figure 29

The *Healthy* Strategy Map©

FINANCIAL
- Opportunity Costs (eg. Revenues)
- Human Capital (HR) Cost Index

CUSTOMER
- Performance on Key Employee Attributes

INTERNAL PROCESSES
- Health/Safety/HR Processes

LEARNING & GROWTH
- Capability/Wellbeing Index©
- Health/Safety (HR) Outcomes Index

Copyright Healthy Business Inc., 2001.

144   Chapter 6 Linking Health into The Balanced Scorecard

For organizations with predictive scorecards, health is a simple, and highly profitable plug-in.

Organizations which can map out this relationship—and measure it—already have the basic pathway in place (Fig. 30):

Figure 30

The Employee-Customer-Profit Chain

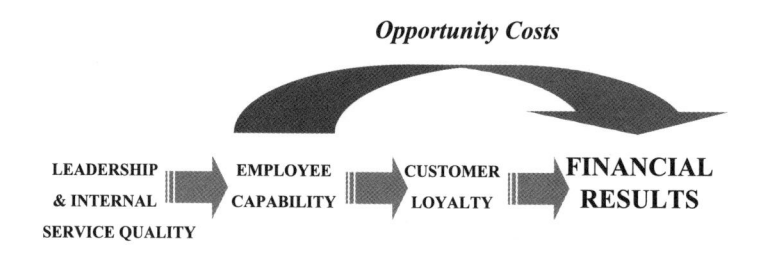

Opportunity Costs

LEADERSHIP & INTERNAL SERVICE QUALITY → EMPLOYEE CAPABILITY → CUSTOMER LOYALTY → **FINANCIAL RESULTS**

But now adding health to the prior equation adds a new dimension to performance improvement. Not only does this substantially enhance customer results, it also adds the direct, indirect, and opportunity impact of health costs. The pathway for this new improvement opportunity, the Healthy Profit Chain©, looks like this:

Figure 31

The Healthy Profit Chain©

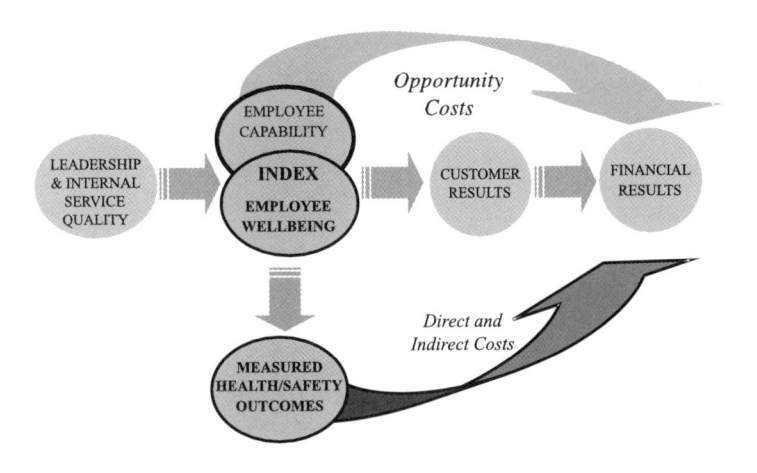

©Healthy Business Inc., 2001

Prerequisite #3

The final criterion for an effective Capability/Wellbeing Index is that it must reflect emerging priorities.

But we first need a starting point. Sears Roebuck took eighteen months of statistical analysis to arrive at ten questions that closely mirror the Gallup *Q^{12} Advantage*.[195] *The Gallup Organization* interviewed over a million employees and 80,000 high performance leaders to arrive at their top-12 questions.[196]

Surely individual workplaces can jump-start the process by learning from the best? Further, given the need for brevity in quarterly employee measures, it seems logical for us to benchmark. So a generic index can be a very helpful stepping stone for your measurement initiative. But it should not be the end point.

A helpful way to look at changes in the Capability/Wellbeing Index is to consider Maslow's Hierarchy of Needs (Fig. 32). Abraham Maslow is widely recognized for his work to identify the basic motivators of human performance.

> *"Human life will never be understood unless its highest aspirations are taken into account. Growth, self-actualization, the striving toward health, the quest for identity and autonomy, the yearning for excellence... must by now be accepted beyond question as a widespread and perhaps universal human tendency."*
>
> Abraham Maslow
> *Motivation and Personality*[197]

Figure 32

Maslow's Hierarchy of Needs

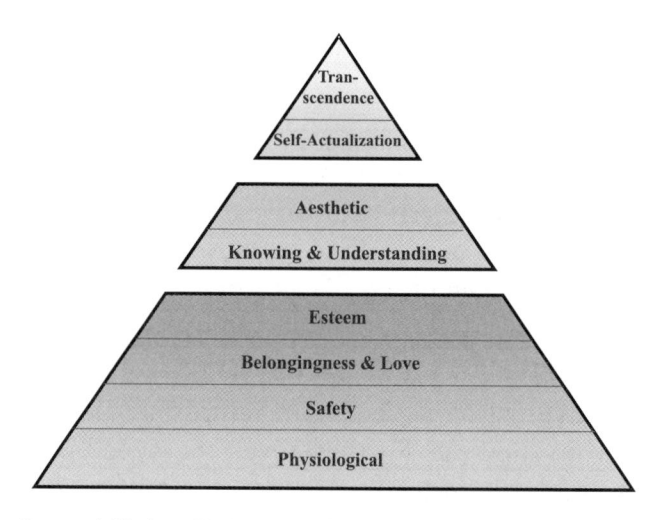

- Transcendence
- Self-Actualization
- Aesthetic
- Knowing & Understanding
- Esteem
- Belongingness & Love
- Safety
- Physiological

Source: A Maslow, *Motivation and Personality*, New York, 1954.

Maslow set the stage for fluid human capital measurement by acknowledging that needs change, and that as more basic needs are met, others take precedence.

This dovetails beautifully with the premise of Drs. Kaplan and Norton—that the Balanced Scorecard is not a static tool, but an evolving process.

For those of you who have camped in the Canadian Rockies—this shifting hierarchy will be familiar. When you're out in the wilderness, the desire for a midnight snack in the tent is overridden by the desire not to be eaten by a grizzly bear. So a granola treat or a Bailey's nightcap in the tent—an aesthetic need—is off-limits, *verboten* [198] due to the more basic need for survival. But on returning safe and sound at home, it's open season on late-night snacks.

The same shift in priorities happens in the workplace. Just like peeling an onion, as leaders address pressing issues, others surface. With our new understanding of the drivers of health, we can ensure that our employee indices capture the basics. But we can—and should—also finesse the Capability/Wellbeing Index to reflect emerging priorities.

Balancing Measures: Importance versus Performance

One way to identify changing priorities is to balance measures according to relative importance and relative performance. Federal Express reshaped their "*Hierarchy of Horrors*", the most frequently cited customer complaints, by teasing out which were the most important. Specifically, they identified the most important service areas with the highest performance gaps.[199] These Service/Quality Indicators (Fig. 33) help employees understand customer service priorities:

Figure 33

Federal Express Service/Quality Indicators[200]

Sample Indicator	Weight
Lost packages	50
Damaged packages	30
Complaints reopened	10
Wrong Day Late Deliveries	10
Right day late deliveries	1
Abandoned calls	1

Source: American Management Association, *Blueprints for Service Quality: The Federal Express Approach*, 1977.

This kind of weighting system serves as an excellent learning tool for the service dimensions which really matter. And this can be applied to employee measures as well.

The U.S. Department of Transportation (DOT) balances their 12-point survey according to relative importance and relative performance. This helps them to stay abreast of employee needs and changing improvement priorities. And it provides a quick-and-dirty means for them to calibrate their employee index.[201]

By linking their mini-survey with their intranet, the DOT has created a vehicle which is convenient for the user, as well as for the data-crunchers. Users can tap into the site and complete the survey within five minutes. And programmers can set up analysis in advance, so results are calculated and displayed with ease. This is a far cry from the posse of 18 data-entry personnel required by one of my earlier clients to input their survey results.

Figure 34

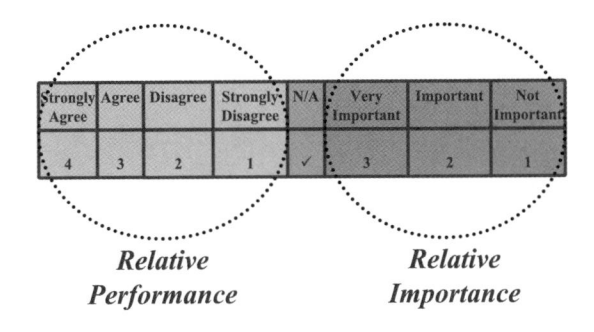

Balancing Measures with a Web-Based Survey

Strongly Agree	Agree	Disagree	Strongly Disagree	N/A	Very Important	Important	Not Important
4	3	2	1	✓	3	2	1

Relative Performance   *Relative Importance*

Source: U.S. Department of Transportation survey: http//pie.dot.gov/pie/DEMO.

Mark Henderson, Executive Vice President of the Clemmer Group, uses the following model (Fig. 35) to balance performance measures.[202] This provides a handy decision support to assist in the allocation of limited resources to strategically important initiatives. Like the Balanced Scorecard, balanced measures assist organizations to identify improvement priorities, and to reallocate funds from nonessential areas.

The hiccup in this approach is to differentiate what employees say from what they do.

In my earlier years when I worked as a physiotherapist, patients would come into my office and say, "*I have a sore hand, fix my hand.*" I'd treat their neck and the hand pain would go away. Our leaders face the same mismatch between wants and needs. Many leaders know what they *want* to make a workplace healthy, but they don't know what they *need*.

Figure 35

Balanced Measures Focus Priority Improvement Efforts

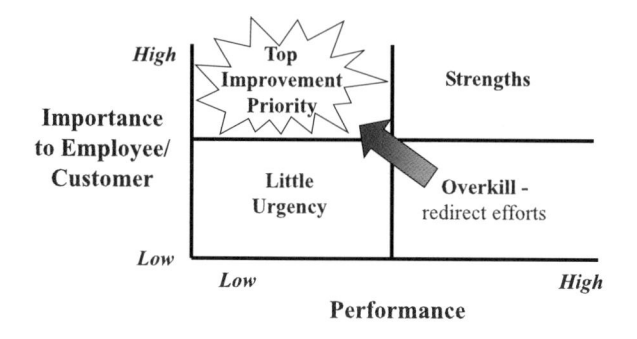

```
Importance      High │  Top          │
to Employee/         │  Improvement  │  Strengths
Customer             │  Priority     │
                     ├───────────────┼──────────────
                     │               │  Overkill -
                     │  Little       │  redirect efforts
                     │  Urgency      │
                Low  └───────────────┴──────────────
                     Low                        High
                           Performance
```

Source: Mark Henderson, Executive Vice President, The Clemmer Group

So this method of balancing performance measures must be used judiciously, since improvement efforts deemed "*Very important*" may not in fact be the ones which drive superior business or health outcomes.

Calibrating the Capability/Wellbeing Index

Many organizations conduct a temperature check every couple of years—an employee survey. The problem with biannual surveys is that many organizations rely on these alone for employee feedback. And the temptation in annual or biannual surveys is to survey the moon. No wonder that employees feel jaded if they have to take the time to answer 150 survey questions (particularly if the results are neither reported, nor acted upon). If this is your only employee survey tool, it yields sluggish and dated results, at best.

Turns out that *regular* surveying is tightly linked with the quality of your Human Resources System, and in turn with your stock performance. At a recent Balanced Scorecard Collaborative NetConference on the HR Scorecard, researchers Brian Becker and Mark Huselid shared from their research that in the bottom 10% of Human Resources Systems, only 5% of organizations measure employee opinion frequently; in the top 10%, it's 58%. It's not surprising that organizations are turning to effective feedback loops to strengthen their performance results. And that's ultimately what the Healthy Scorecard offers.

What's Wrong with Biannual Measurements?

Ask any emergency room physician on the wisdom of biannual temperature checks, and they'll point to two problems:

1) *You can't assess which treatments work when you only measure their effects every two years; and,*
2) *The patient might die.*

Such is the case with organizational culture and health outcomes. What is begging to be done (cheaply and simply!) is to finesse existing quarterly employee mini-surveys to capture the cultural drivers of capability so that we can respond to them in an intelligent and timely fashion.

Once you've embarked on a generic Capability/Wellbeing Index, you have the opportunity to mould it to your unique environment. Results from a biannual survey are still very helpful in shaping priorities for the evolving Capability/Wellbeing Index.

If the quarterly Index is 10-15 questions, individual business units should be given latitude to add a 2-3 questions to reflect their unique needs. This is being explored in the five pilot business units implementing the Balanced Scorecard at the City of Calgary.

The Business Health Culture Index©[203]

Dr. Martin Shain, Head of the Workplace Program at the Centre for Addiction and Mental Health provides another twist which could be readily incorporated into a Capability/Wellbeing Index. Dr. Shain's expertise is sought at the highest levels in Canadian corporations, and he spearheads Health Canada's workplace health research innovations.

Dr. Shain has created an extraordinarily concise, powerful, and practical tool to measure upstream health drivers. The Business Health Culture Index captures four of the key upstream indicators: effort/reward, and demand/control. This index lends itself beautifully to the Healthy Scorecard process.

Dr. Shain describes this index, and the Health Canada research on which it is based, in the inset on the following page.

THE BUSINESS HEALTH CULTURE INDEX©
by Dr. Martin Shain[204]

Recently, in a series of workplace surveys of employee health, we had the opportunity to redefine the way in which demand relates to control, and effort relates to reward by constructing a Business Health Culture Index in which markers of demand and effort were seen as Stressors, and markers of control and reward were seen as Satisfiers. We were then able to assign every employee who took part in the survey a score based on the relationship between these specific stressors and these specific satisfiers in their particular work life.

The Business Health Culture Index (BHCI) yields essential information about the ratio between stress (demand/effort) and satisfaction (control/reward) at an individual and collective level. The BCHI is constructed from aggregate business unit or organization-wide answers to four simple questions in the (Health Canada) employee health survey, yielding two subscores and a final score derived from them, as follows:

Satisfaction Subscore:

*1) I feel I am well **rewarded** for the level of effort I put out for my job.*

*2) I am satisfied with the amount of **involvement** I have in decisions that affect my work.*

Stress Subscore:

1) Work stress in the last six months from too much time pressure (✓ -2 to +2)

2) Work stress in the last six months from mental fatigue (✓ -2 to +2)

The BHCI is a reflection of upstream *drivers* of downstream health related costs which themselves are typically measured through *indicators* such as absenteeism, injuries, insurance claims, and use of services such as employee and family assistance programs.

Increasingly, we see close relationships between BHCIs and customer satisfaction indicators.

From *Investing in Comprehensive Workplace Health Promotion*, Health Canada, December 2000. © Minister of Public Works and Government Services Canada, 2001.

Dr. Shain's work hits the nail on the head. And while there will always be time to finesse such an index, it provides us with a running start. Organizations which use tools such as the *Q¹² Advantage®* can simply plug in the questions from the Business Health Culture Index, to tap into lasting and healthy business results.

The Multiple Health Risk Score©[205]

If strategy is a series of cause and effect relationships, then Dr. Shain is providing the dots for us to link. Another tool he has used with the City of Calgary is the Multiple Health Risk Score©, a composite of six potential risk factors which have powerful impact on organizational outcomes such as absenteeism. The six risks are:

- Physical Activity
- Body mass index
- Trouble sleeping
- Nutrition
- Smoking; and
- Alcohol consumption.

Employees are grouped into Low Risk, Moderate Risk, and High Risk groups according to how many of these risk factors they have. At the City of Calgary, 78% of employees currently fall into the moderate and high risk groups.[206] And these risk factors pack a punch!

As illustrated in Figure 36, moderate and high risk employees experience substantially higher absenteeism than their low risk counterparts. In fact, absenteeism is increased in these groups by a factor of *three*!

Figure 36

How Health Risk Profile affects Absenteeism due to Illness

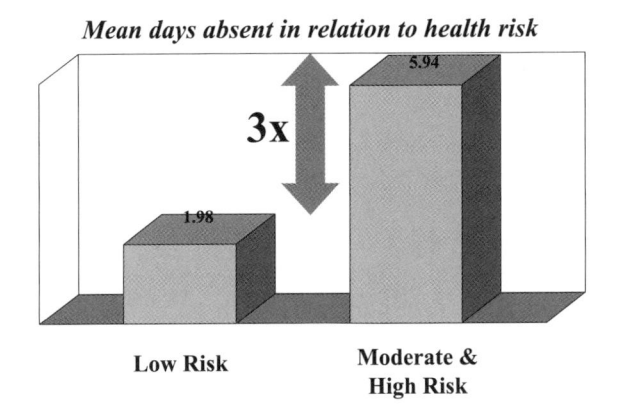

Mean days absent in relation to health risk

- Low Risk: 1.98
- Moderate & High Risk: 5.94
- 3x difference

Source: Martin Law, Presentation to World Mental Health Conference, *"Wellness at the City of Calgary"*, October 5, 2000.

Let's take a look at one of these six risk factors to illustrate how we can capture cause and effect between leadership and health/financial outcomes.

We'll focus on a popular (or should I say notorious!) topic: sleep.

How management quality affects employee sleep patterns

Now there are many factors which can cause people to have difficulty sleeping. But a *major* factor for employees is the caliber of their immediate supervisor. The St. Paul Fire and Marine Insurance company found that employees who reported having an unsupportive supervisor were more than two times as likely to experience sleep problems.[207]

What does this mean for employee health? Well, psychologist Dr. Stanley Coren tells us that if you have difficulty sleeping, you are more than twice as likely to visit your physician (Fig. 37)—which health professionals will readily agree typically translates into a prescription for medication.[208] It is widely accepted that if you are sleep-deprived, your immune system can become suppressed, and your tissue healing become impaired. Enter the field of "psychoneuroimmunology"— the mind/body link.

Figure 37

Sleep and Health Care Utilization

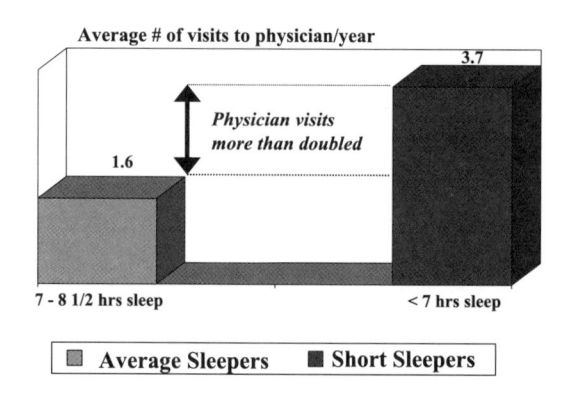

Average # of visits to physician/year

3.7

1.6

Physician visits more than doubled

7 - 8 1/2 hrs sleep   < 7 hrs sleep

▨ Average Sleepers   ■ Short Sleepers

Source: Coren S., *Sleep Thieves*, Free Press, Toronto, 1996.

So we can see a pattern emerging from leadership quality, to employee health risk profile, to organizational and health outcomes (such as absenteeism), and health cost outcomes (such as drug costs).

Far from being depressing news, this is great news! Employee health is not just something which happens in a vacuum. Leaders can directly—and profoundly—influence outcomes.

A Closer Look at the Healthy Corporate Scorecard

Now let's take a closer look at how to embed wellbeing within the corporate scorecard. One of the important ingredients in a healthy corporate scorecard is our accounting method: Total Cost of Health accounting.[209]

*If you want to show cause-and-effect in your BSC, and capture the spin-off health benefits of a capable and engaged workforce, then you **must** steer clear of silo accounting.*

Drill-Down Example: Employee Stress

To begin, let's take a look at a hot potato for workplace health: employee stress. And let's also take on a financial headache: rising prescription drug costs. Now let's see how we can address these in a corporate scorecard.

1) Understand how Leadership affects Medication Use

First we'll start with a snapshot of how the quality of the work environment affects depression and prescription drug use. Two of my favorite examples come from Robert Karasek and Töres Theorell's pioneering book, *Healthy Work*.[210] These two images, from research on Swedish Males, and U.S. females,[211] speak volumes for the pivotal role of leaders in employee health.[212]

As job demands increase, and employee decision latitude (or control over how work is done) decreases, depression (Fig. 38) and pill consumption (Fig. 39) both increase.

Figure 38

Job Characteristics and Depression – U.S. Females

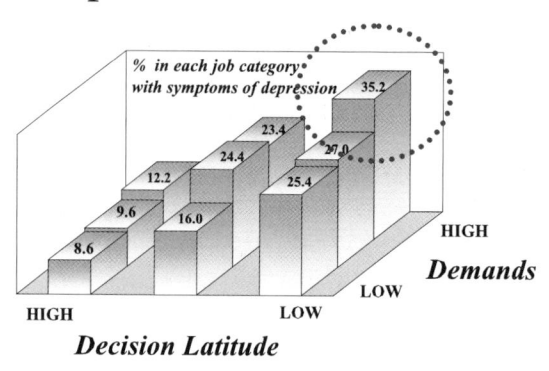

% in each job category with symptoms of depression

8.6, 9.6, 12.2, 16.0, 24.4, 25.4, 23.4, 29.0, 35.2

Decision Latitude: HIGH — LOW
Demands: HIGH — LOW

Source: U.S. Quality of Employment Surveys, 1972, 1977, as cited by Karasek R., Theorell T., *Healthy Work*, Basic Books, 1990. Reproduced with permission from the authors.

These powerful images suggest that we can dramatically reduce depression and pill consumption, merely by improving the quality of the work environment.

Figure 39

Job Characteristics and Pill Consumption

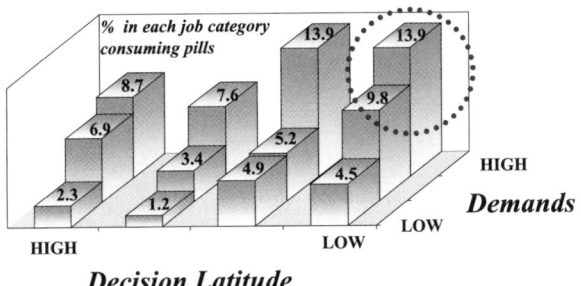

% in each job category consuming pills

	HIGH Demands		LOW Demands
HIGH Decision Latitude	2.3 / 6.9 / 8.7		
	1.2 / 3.4 / 7.6		
	4.9 / 5.2 / 13.9		
LOW Decision Latitude	4.5 / 9.8 / 13.9		

Values shown in chart: 2.3, 6.9, 8.7, 1.2, 3.4, 7.6, 4.9, 5.2, 13.9, 4.5, 9.8, 13.9

Source: Swedish Males, 1968, from Karasek R., Theorell, T., *Healthy Work*, Basic Books, 1990. Reproduced with permission from the authors.

One way we might do this is to reduce red tape the way that Jack Welch did at GE in the 1980's with his *"Dumb Rules and Forms Committee"*, which systematically rooted out bureaucratic logjams. Similarly, Washington Governor Gary Locke recently repealed 6,550 administrative rules, and tore up more than 2000 pages following his executive order in 1997.[213] And you could capture these red-tape busting initiatives with a key process measure.

In the first chapters of this book, I emphasized the need for us to get out of a panic mode when addressing health strategy. Understanding the above dynamic is a vital first step in this quest.

2) Include Key Stressors in Capability/Wellbeing Index

Next, we ensure that our Capability/Wellbeing Index captures at least the Demand/Control and Effort/Reward dimensions— key drivers of both employee capability and wellbeing.

3) *Build a Model for the Total Cost of Stress*

Then we build a fledgling model for the **Total Cost of Stress**: prevention, detection, and failure costs.

- ➤ **Prevention costs** might include: the incremental cost for leadership development initiatives; dispute resolution, conflict mediation, and problem-solving training; process improvements such as red-tape reduction initiatives; education in the appropriate use of medications; or employee health interventions to minimize the severity of problems encountered.

- ➤ **Detection costs** might include health risk appraisals; health screening to detect under-treatment of medical conditions; the cost to administer a quarterly Capability/Wellbeing Index, or employee productivity lost from completing surveys during work hours.

- ➤ **Failure costs** are divided into direct, indirect, and opportunity cost categories, as discussed in Chapter 5—and we can now capture these with the Healthy Scorecard.

4) *Connect the dots*

There is a great deal of interest and concern regarding escalating drug costs. And in my work with the City of Calgary, we have found a partner that can help us prove our impact on stress and the bottom line. Glaxo Wellcome Inc. (GW) has a remarkable decision support tool called *Health Evidence®*, which we are using to capture stress-related drug costs. Beginning with a generic profile of the City's drug utilization,[214]

GW works backwards, using a combination of databases from the Canadian Disease and Therapeutic Index (CDTI) from IMS Health, Canada to arrive at diagnostic profiles for the City.

For example, the CDTI database tells us that the typical prescription pattern for Tylenol 3 is 29% for back disorders, 20% for joint disorders ... and .05% for migraines.[215] We also know that back pain and migraines can be triggered by stress.

Working backwards from the City's drug utilization profile, we apply *Health Evidence*® to arrive at an estimate of what the net stress-related drug cost is for the City.

This is where it gets fun. Now we can feed this up into a Total Cost of Health Index for the City's top five health priorities. A single snapshot already tells us that some business units have much better leadership, morale, and health profiles than others. But it is the longitudinal data which hits our message home.

For example, we can measure the impact across business units, which the City's Corporate Leadership Development Program has on the Capability/Wellbeing Index. We can see how quickly the benefits of the Leadership program take root. We can track the impact this has on stress-related health outcomes such as absenteeism and drug utilization. We can show a link with process, and customer results. And we can show the impact on stress-related drug costs, when the Capability/Wellbeing Index improves.

Finally, we can evaluate the net impact of our intervention on Total Stress Costs, and roll this together with the City's other 4-5 key health issues into the Total Cost of Health Index reported on the HR Cost Index on the corporate scorecard.

This is far more informative than our passive accounting style, which tells us that benefit costs went up 15% in a given year. More to the point is the question, "*What did that increase buy us?*". And how substantially did that affect our capacity for sustained growth? Bottom line, we can show that up-front investment yields huge dividends for employee wellbeing,

162   Chapter 6 Linking Health into The Balanced Scorecard

customer, and financial results.

In the following table (Fig. 40), I map out how we can track stress on the corporate scorecard. You can see the flow from the Capability/Wellbeing Index and Internal Processes, through to health outcomes, and the HR Cost Index on the corporate scorecard. Clearly strategic measures need to be added to this scorecard. But what the figure reveals is how we can, indeed, build scorecards from the bottom-up, and not just the top-down.

Figure 40

Tracking Stress on the Corporate Scorecard

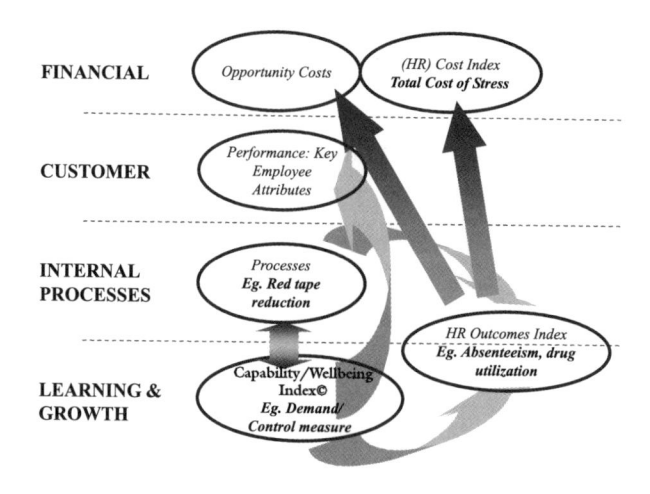

FINANCIAL	Opportunity Costs / (HR) Cost Index Total Cost of Stress
CUSTOMER	Performance: Key Employee Attributes
INTERNAL PROCESSES	Processes Eg. Red tape reduction
LEARNING & GROWTH	Capability/Wellbeing Index© Eg. Demand/Control measure / HR Outcomes Index Eg. Absenteeism, drug utilization

For organizations seriously concerned about spiraling health costs—and high performance—the first step must be to understand prevention.

Drill-Down: Total Cost of Health Index

Now we can begin to intelligently capture cause and effect for the major health issues in your organization. The City of Calgary's Wellness Team, for example, has identified the following broad groups for their first Cost of Health Index:

1) Asthma

2) Hypertension

3) Stress

4) Musculoskeletal Injuries, and

5) Repetitive Strain Injuries.[216]

We are working on Total Cost of Health measures for each of these groups. And these costs will then be rolled into the Total Cost of Health Index.

We expect the composition of the broad Cost of Health Index to change over time. Asthma, for example, is a quick hit.[217] We know this from evidence-based research, such as that from Canada's Community Asthma Care Centres (Fig. 41), which report impressive benefits, a mere six months after intervention.

We know from evidence-based best practices how to manage asthma, and we know that once we get appropriate treatment for the City's employees, patient outcomes will significantly improve, and Total Costs for this category will plummet. We can then turn our attention to the next most pressing health issue, and recalibrate our Total Cost of Health index. This process embodies the type of double-loop learning which Drs. Kaplan and Norton describe in *The Strategy-Focused Organization*.[219] We must not only manage the operations loop, but also improve our strategy and our measures as our needs change, and our understanding of value creation and cost containment improves.

Figure 41

Success and the Community Asthma Care Centres Reducing the Total Cost of Asthma[201]

Outcomes	Percentage Change Adults (17 + years)	Percentage Change Children (< 17 years)
Decline in emergency room visits	78%	73%
Decline in hospital visits	59%	85%
Reduction in hospital lengths of stay	43%	32%
Fewer physician visits	45%	48%
Fewer days lost at work	67%	N/A
Fewer days lost at school	N/A	73%
Fewer days lost by parent at work due to children's asthma	71%	N/A

Source: Community Asthma Care Centres, *Op. Cit.*

What is important is that we remain true to the intent of the Balanced Scorecard, and demonstrate cause-and-effect in our accounting for health.

Accounting for Health in a Human Capital Cost Index

I suggest that many scorecards have—or soon will have—an index to capture human capital costs in the Financial perspective of their Balanced Scorecard. With a War for Talent, a groundswell of interest in human capital measurement, and two outstanding books on the HR Scorecard arriving on the scene,[220] [221] it is only a matter of time before these measures become prevalent.

So let me show you how the Total Cost of Health fits within a Human Capital Cost Index: (Fig. 42)

Those of you familiar with Verizon's award-winning Human Resources Scorecard[222] will recognize the cascading nature of indices to raw measures. What is important in this model is that Human Capital *risk* be separate and distinct from Human Capital *investment*. For example, we approach investment in training very differently from the cost of turnover. To optimize the investment side, we may well want to increase it. To optimize the risk side, we of course want to reduce Total Costs.

Under the Health and Safety cost cell in Figure 42, there are two options:

1) The traditional approach to silo health accounting; and
2) The preferred Total Cost of Health approach.

By mapping out the Top 5 Health Issues, and the Total Cost of Health profile for each issue, leaders become familiar with the data needs for cause-and-effect accounting. This assists leaders to understand our impact on employee health and business results. The strategy map then links health with corporate strategy.

Finally, we want to identify which measures we can currently capture, and which ones we want to capture in the future.

166 Chapter 6 Linking Health into The Balanced Scorecard

Figure 42

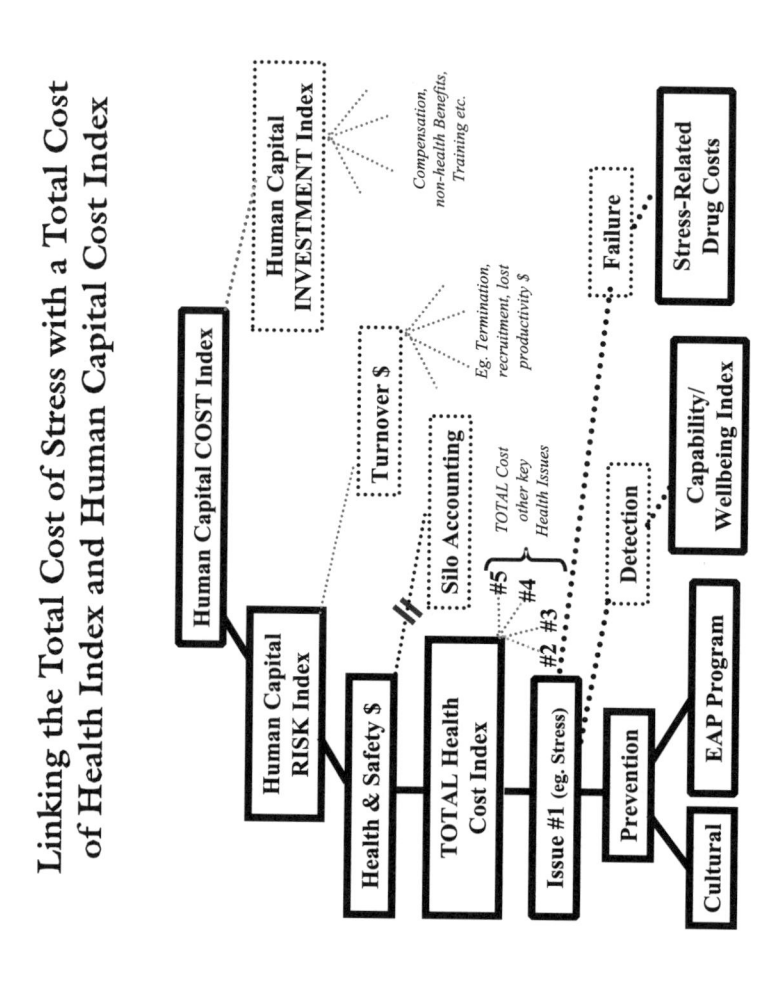

COLOR-CODING YOUR MEASUREMENT STRATEGY

"The Balanced Scorecard should not be driven by the data that is available."

Herb Zagarow
CEO, Quality Alert Institute[223]

So what does a healthy scorecard look like in practice? Many users are familiar with the red-orange-green colors used to report performance on a BSC. Typically, green results reflect superior performance, orange reflect satisfactory performance, and red reflect high-priority improvement areas. This provides a quick visual report card on performance for managers and employees.

But there's another way to color code the scorecard, and I have found this exceptionally helpful in building executive understanding for health strategy. The State of Washington uses a color-coding system to reflect the *state of readiness* for their measures.[224] From green data—which we have—to red data—which we don't have but eventually want—this is truly a wonderful and simple tool to illustrate your measurement strategy.

The challenge in building health into the Balanced Scorecard is to move from measures that we have, to measures that we need.

Figure 43

Mapping out the Measurement Strategy: State of Washington's Color-Coding

- GREEN = data definition is clear, data being collected

- YELLOW = no data/poor quality data with plan to improve

- **RED** = no data and no plan yet to develop

- MIXED = different sources/differing states of readiness

Source: Rene Ewing, State of Washington, BSC for Government 2,000 Conference, Washington D.C., 2000.

The State of Washington's color-coding system enables us to paint a strategic vision of where we are going with our human capital measurement, and to temper this with the reality of what we have. Mapped out on an evolving scorecard for Calgary Transit (Fig. 44), the measurement plan provides an instant visual of where we are, and where we are going.[225] (In this particular example, you will note that Learning and Growth have been separated from the Employee perspective. I have difficulty with this separation—since capability and wellbeing measures flow across both areas. For example, I think of "Building a Learning Organization" (Objective L1), and "Improving Employee Capability/Wellbeing" (Objective E2) as two sides of the same coin.)

To give you some context for the scorecard on the next page: The normal font objectives are those cascaded down from the City of Calgary's Corporate Balanced Scorecard. The italicized objectives are unique objectives developed by Calgary Transit. The dark shaded boxes represent "green" measures which we already have data for. The medium shaded boxes represent "orange" measures which need some work. And the lightly spotted box represents a "red" measure which we feel must ultimately be developed.

Let's take a closer look at our color-coding for our health measures. The green measures we already have. The red measures we have in our crosshairs for the future. The wellbeing measures that we're currently working on—the orange measures—include:

- Human Capital Risk Index (F2a)
- Employee Safety Index (P3b); and
- Overtime Risk Index (E2c)[226]

To show how we apply color-coding, let's take a look at the Internal Process Perspective in Figure 44, Objective P3: *Safety*. Calgary Transit strategically targets safety improvements for their employees, customers, and their vehicles—the transit fleet. Employee safety is the focus in the following example.

Example: An Employee Safety Index

Let me share with you our rationale for the Employee Safety Index. Currently managers at Calgary Transit are familiar with Employee Injury Rate (Lost time injury frequency) as a proxy for employee safety. This is a green measure. We have numbers for it, and the executive team understands it. But the Wellness Team would ultimately like to move to a more comprehensive and meaningful index.

170 Chapter 6 Linking Health into The Balanced Scorecard

Figure 44

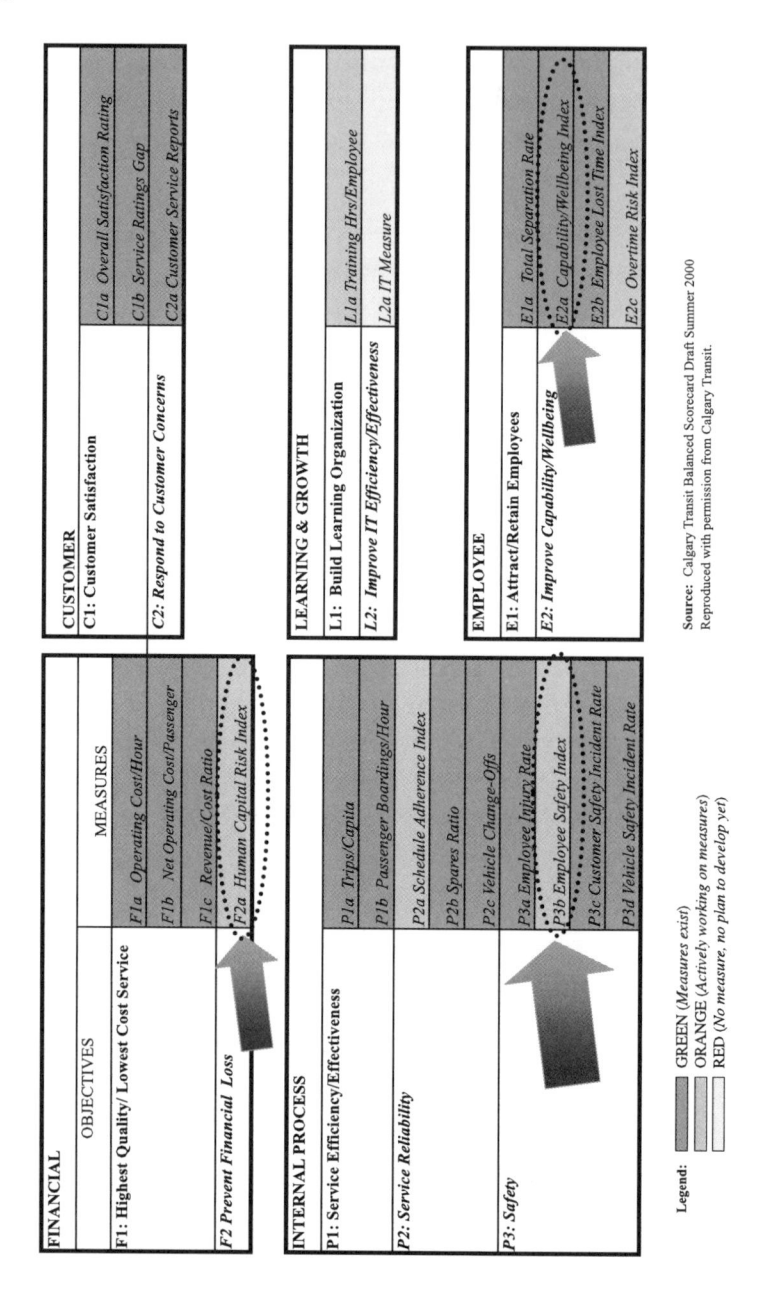

FINANCIAL

OBJECTIVES	MEASURES
F1: Highest Quality/ Lowest Cost Service	F1a Operating Cost/Hour
	F1b Net Operating Cost/Passenger
	F1c Revenue/Cost Ratio
F2 Prevent Financial Loss	F2a Human Capital Risk Index

CUSTOMER

C1: Customer Satisfaction	C1a Overall Satisfaction Rating
	C1b Service Ratings Gap
C2: Respond to Customer Concerns	C2a Customer Service Reports

INTERNAL PROCESS

P1: Service Efficiency/Effectiveness	P1a Trips/Capita
	P1b Passenger Boardings/Hour
P2: Service Reliability	P2a Schedule Adherence Index
	P2b Spares Ratio
	P2c Vehicle Change-Offs
P3: Safety	P3a Employee Injury Rate
	P3b Employee Safety Index
	P3c Customer Safety Incident Rate
	P3d Vehicle Safety Incident Rate

LEARNING & GROWTH

L1: Build Learning Organization	L1a Training Hrs/Employee
L2: Improve IT Efficiency/Effectiveness	L2a IT Measure

EMPLOYEE

E1: Attract/Retain Employees	E1a Total Separation Rate
E2: Improve Capability/Wellbeing	E2a Capability/Wellbeing Index
	E2b Employee Lost Time Index
	E2c Overtime Risk Index

Legend:
- GREEN *(Measures exist)*
- ORANGE *(Actively working on measures)*
- RED *(No measure, no plan to develop yet)*

Source: Calgary Transit Balanced Scorecard Draft Summer 2000
Reproduced with permission from Calgary Transit.

In the context of an aging population (the average age for City employees is 44), effective rehabilitation and return to work are as important strategically as preventing injuries in the first place. So simply reporting injury rates on the scorecard can be misleading. We are envisioning an Employee Safety Index, to capture:

- Injury event rates
- Injury severity (average days lost/event); and
- Rehabilitation success.

These measures in turn will be broken down into on-the-job measures, and off-the-job measures . (Fig. 45)

Martin Lesperance, firefighter/paramedic and acclaimed speaker on off-the-job safety notes that off-the-job injuries for many of his corporate clients outnumber work-related injuries by a factor of ten to one.[227] In fact, one of his major oil and gas clients recently analyzed their lost time days for the past three years, and found that 95% of these were nonoccupational![228] It makes sense that any measure of injury rates includes off-the-job, as well as on-the-job statistics.

Similarly, Dave Denoon HR Consultant with the City of Calgary's Wellness Team notes that participation by injured employees in the City's Occupational Injury Services (OIS) is a powerful leading indicator for favorable rehabilitation outcomes. OIS focuses on work-related injuries, and gets employees back to work more quickly than other options. So the percentage of injured City employees receiving treatment through the Occupational Injury Services is an important leading indicator of safety outcomes.

Finally, "Stick Rates", or the percentage of employees returning to work who actually stay at work—are an important measure. Having treated patients at Worker's Compensation clinics, I can attest to the fragility of return-to-work successes. Simply returning employees to work is not enough if they go back on disability the next week.

Figure 45 shows how we ultimately plan to roll up these key indicators into a Safety Index. Again timing will be important. This kind of index can merely confuse managers coping with a new Balanced Scorecard, or a new understanding of safety drivers. But once managers have their Balanced Scorecard sea legs, the index will be a much more meaningful measure of safety success.

Figure 45

Creating more Effective Measures
The Employee Safety Index

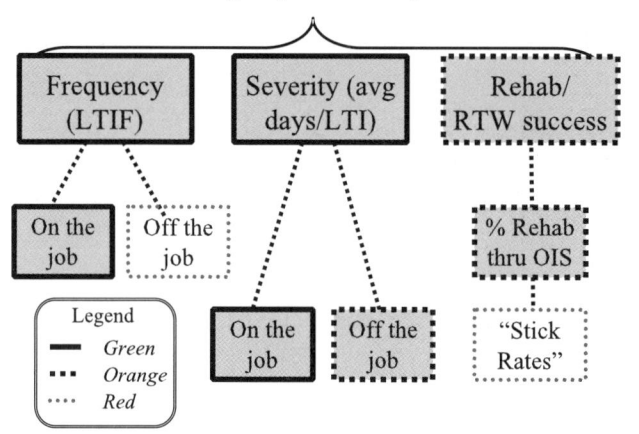

Frequency (LTIF)	Severity (avg days/LTI)	Rehab/ RTW success

- On the job / Off the job
- On the job / Off the job
- % Rehab thru OIS
- "Stick Rates"

Legend
— Green
··· Orange
···· Red

BUILDING ALIGNMENT

> *"Alignment gives you the power to get and stay competitive by bringing together previously unconnected parts of your organization into an interrelated, easily comprehensible model."*
>
> George Labovitz and Victor Rosansky
> *The Power of Alignment*[229]

One of the most profound challenges in the New Economy will be to build strategic alignment for employee wellbeing. And this will be no small feat, given the widespread misinformation regarding health drivers. Health, safety, wellbeing—call it what you want—is viewed as a frill, if not downright flaky. It is nothing short of heresy for those entrenched in "hard" numbers, to say that employee wellbeing drives superior and sustained stock performance. But—as the fairytale character Rumpelstiltskin would say—it does. Who will exercise the necessary leadership to act on this information, and hold managers accountable for event rates in health outcomes, as well as productivity and profits?

Leading organizations have aligned their improvement initiatives with process quality. Some, such as Federal Express build accountability for employee satisfaction, and action on employee survey findings.[230] The Bank of Montreal is moving in a similar direction to hold leaders accountable for employee results. In this case, managers are given flexibility to identify employee measures that they feel they can impact.[231]

The next step in human capital management is to link incentive compensation with health, as well as employee, customer, and financial results.

I also have to wonder what the legal implications will be when corporations recognize that they have a direct and profound impact on employee wellbeing. What will corporate legal engines do with this? The head-in-the-sand approach might be to avoid measuring cause-and-effect for employee wellbeing, for fear of reprisals.

> *But a can of worms is still a can of worms—*
> *even if you don't open it.*

I'm looking forward to the gutsy organizations which acknowledge the shared opportunity for leaders—together with employees and their families—to create spectacular improvements in organizational health.

The topic of alignment for organizational health provides enough material for an entire book. And wellbeing is such a new topic to the Balanced Scorecard that a full exploration is premature. Suffice it to say that if you hold your leaders truly accountable for results in the Capability/Wellbeing Index, as well as key health indices on the corporate scorecard, your results will open a new frontier in sustainable high performance.

BUILDING NIMBLENESS

One of the most exciting outcomes that you can expect from building a Healthy Scorecard is organizational *nimbleness* to respond to the soft results that matter. So the true value-add of the Healthy Scorecard is not in the measures *per se*, but in the responsive cycle of inquiry and action which it generates. This innovation capital, as Skandia terms it, drives our ability to meet the pace of global business demands.[232] Let's take a look at some of the decision support tools which can accelerate our learning curve.

Hewitt's HR Action Centre

Hewitt & Associates just released their "*HR Action Centre*", a decision support tool which houses a wealth of research on human resources best practices. This tool can be linked with enterprise management software such as PeopleSoft to "pull" managers to the supports they need. In this way, small organizations can benefit from the learning of the statistically correct behemoths.

Let's suppose that you are a manager who has just scored poorly on communicating with employees. Your communication results would show up as red on your Balanced Scorecard. At a click of a button, the HR Action Centre would target your strategic learning needs, and link you with best practices in communication skill development.[233]

The Sears Intranet: Best Practices

Sears Roebuck has built this kind of capability internally. Their intranet hosts a dazzling array of learning supports on their Success Sharing site. Managers can type in "*Store like me*", and find another business unit with similar characteristics. They can then learn how other stores address similar challenges. Managers can drill down through a wealth of best practices to find the specific supports they need. In short, Sears can now *accelerate* cycle time for leadership development.[234]

How Quickly can we turn around Organizational Health?

The winners in Balanced Scorecard implementation are proving the cause and effect linkages between satisfied and capable employees, a flexible/adaptive work environment, and process, customer, and financial results. And they are achieving spectacular turnarounds!

In fact, Balanced Scorecard turnarounds are happening in the first year. For example, Chemical Bank, one of the early adopters of the BSC, increased their profits by a factor of eight in one year, when they implemented their BSC in 1993.[235]

These turnarounds are not limited to the private sector, nor are they limited to financial results. This is good news for executives, employees, and investors.

Figure 46 underscores how quickly organizations can transform their culture. For example, the U.S. Naval Undersea Warfare Centre (NUWC) turned around areas that I would consider to fall into the "meaningful involvement", and "belonging" categories—key drivers of health, safety, and capability outcomes. Between 1996 and 1998, NUWC delivered the following results:

> *"I am sufficiently informed about the Naval Undersea Warfare Centre's strategic plan."* (*"Agrees"* increased from 10% to 83%)

> *"I feel that I have the ability to make a contribution in building NUWC to be an effective 21st Century organization."* (*"Agrees"* increased from 34% to 74%)

To any follower of organizational health research, this also signifies a health turnaround.

Figure 46

Cultural Breakthroughs with the Balanced Scorecard

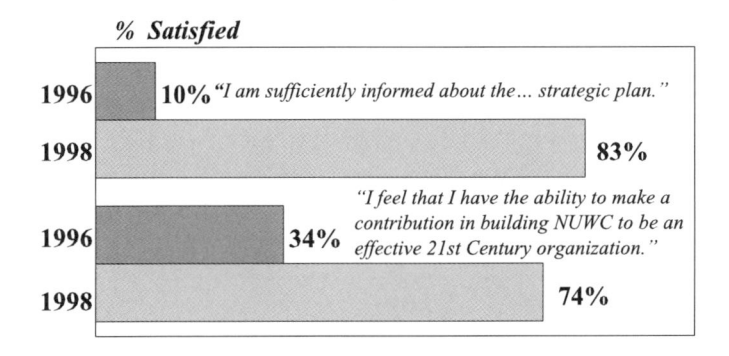

% Satisfied

Year	%	Statement
1996	10%	"I am sufficiently informed about the... strategic plan."
1998	83%	
1996	34%	"I feel that I have the ability to make a contribution in building NUWC to be an effective 21st Century organization."
1998	74%	

Source: Division of Newport, Naval Undersea Warfare Center
BSC for Government 2,000 Conference, Washington D.C., 2,000.

WHAT ABOUT SMALL BUSINESSES?

But what about small businesses? Does size matter?

How can organizations build a predictive BSC when they lack the critical mass to develop statistically valid and reliable *causal* predictions? The answer is, "*They shouldn't*"! The garden variety BSC will do just fine.

Just as early adopters seized on the results of early research in the quality field, so can early leaders in human capital excellence just take the health ball and run with it. If your managers are convinced that good leadership drives health and business outcomes, then "*Just do it*" and act on your convictions. What is important is the open and continuous enquiry toward what produces value—and what creates cost—for your organization.

Small businesses can also capitalize on the best practices of the corporate giants. For example, decision support tools, such as Hewitt & Associate's *HR Action Centre*, enable small businesses to leverage learning on human performance from their corporate peers.

You can wait for more empirical proof that good health is good leadership is great business. I say don't waste your time! The evidence is in, and it's time to act on the opportunity presented by the Healthy Scorecard. In fact, I predict that within the next two years we'll see breakthrough applications with major corporations demonstrating *hundreds of millions* of dollars in cost savings, and value creation from the Healthy Scorecard.

HUMAN RESOURCES, AND HEALTH AND SAFETY SCORECARDS

There are many exciting advances which are pushing the frontiers of strategic health and human capital measurement.

- The Institute for Work and Health in Toronto, Canada[236] is working on a *"Healthy Workplace" Scorecard* to capture the nuances of the organizational health function. This scorecard offers higher resolution for metrics of the health and safety function. Combined with the *Healthy Scorecard*, the Institute's work promises a full spectrum of strategic wellbeing measures, from the executive level, to the workplace health practitioner.
- David Ulrich, Mark Huselid and Brian Becker are deeply involved with Drs. Kaplan and Norton's *Balanced Scorecard Collaborative*, and will be publishing their book on the HR Scorecard this year. Their preliminary work through the

BSC Collaborative provides illuminating insights into HR's role in strategic value creation and cost control.[237]

- Dr. Jack Phillips, head of the Jack Phillips Center for Research, an affiliate of Franklin Covey is also publishing his book this year on the *Human Resources Scorecard: Measuring the Return on Investment.*[238]
- Jac Fitz Enz, author of *The ROI of Human Capital*, and the Saratoga Institute continue to build on their excellent metrics for the HR function.[239]
- The International Quality and Productivity Centre[240] is profiling leaders in human capital measurement at its *HR Measurement conferences.*
- And Skandia continues to trailblaze in Intellectual Capital measurement and strategy.[241]

This work will collectively advance our strategic HR vision.

*My immediate concern however, is to entrench employee wellbeing within the **corporate** scorecard.*

I come back to my earlier premise—that we need not only strategic Human Resource measures on the corporate scorecard, but also *fundamental* human measures that transcend strategy. In fact, I submit that successful strategic execution cannot be *sustained* unless we include these basics.

Since most BSC's begin at the corporate level, it is incumbent on trailblazers to educate leaders how to fit human motivation into the equation, right from the start. The Balanced Scorecard is still new enough that many organizations are still learning to walk. So while the trailblazers break new ground in the intricacies of HR and ROI measurement, we can ensure that corporate scorecards have the basics.

For executives to embrace human capital investments, we need to create living, breathing corporate scorecards, which reinforce, quarter after quarter, the direct and phenomenal contribution of people to business results.

It's high time to connect the dots between great managers, capable and healthy employees, and superior corporate performance.

Let's create a minimum threshold of predictive excellence that all corporate scorecards must live up to. Let's ensure that all Balanced Scorecards are powered by an index which captures the drivers of employee capability *and* wellbeing. Let's build Balanced Scorecards from the bottom-up, as well as the top-down. Let's build the strategic metrics for sustainable growth. In short, let's create scorecards which employees, customers, and investors *demand!*

For us to truly win the War for Talent, we need to get employee wellbeing on the executive radar screen. And that means embedding health strategy within the corporate scorecard. Because many organizations are adopting the BSC to craft their business strategy, our challenge is to demonstrate how employee wellbeing in fact *drives* the Learning and Growth perspective.

How well are you doing this?

LEADERSHIP CHECK-UP

Employee Pulsechecks

1) How frequently do you measure employee attitudes or satisfaction?
2) How quickly can respondents complete the employee survey?
3) What kind of return rates do you have for your employee surveys?

Survey-Feedback-Action[242]

4) How well do you communicate employee results?
    a) How do you know?
5) How well do you act on employee feedback?
    a) How do you know?

Mapping your Strategy

6) Does your employee survey capture the Effort/Reward and Demand/Control dynamics?
7) Do you know what your top five health issues are in your organization?
8) Do you capture Total Health Costs for your top five health issues?
9) Do you link your employee survey results with health outcomes (event rates *and* costs), customer outcomes, value creation, and human capital cost?
10) Does your Strategy Map[243] tell the story of how capable, motivated, and healthy employees contribute to sustained business success?

7

THE BIG PICTURE

THE LEVER FOR CHANGE: INSTITUTIONAL INVESTORS

> *"Institutional investors—like the Council of Institutional Investors, which manages over $1 trillion worth of stocks... define the agenda for the business world. Where they lead, everyone else follows... (they) have started to pay much closer attention to how companies treat their people."*
>
> Buckingham M., Coffman C.
> *First, Break all the Rules*[244]

This book is targeted to senior executives seeking untapped and dramatic improvement opportunities. But I also want to win over institutional investors with a spectacular new way to predict and supercharge future financial performance.

Let me first establish that I'm not interested in generating the kind of short-term stock turnarounds that bleed results. Anybody can cut costs. But not many can cut costs *and* add sustainable value. That's what I'm interested in.

I want superior, low risk, and long-term stock returns. And yes, this is achievable with the Healthy Scorecard!

In fact, the Healthy Scorecard offers a vast untapped field for breakthrough business results. A trillion dollars in health costs—slashed in half—is not the only motivation for us to begin this journey.[245] There's also the value creation that comes from healthy, inspired employees. And as I've noted in this work, we haven't even begun to quantify this health capital value. But we can. And we can reflect this newfound knowledge in our investment strategies.

> *"I would like to challenge all of us to invest with at least a five-year horizon, and preferably 10 or more. And I challenge executives to accept that managing your stock for anything less than a five-to-ten-year horizon confuses price and value, and is — quite simply — irresponsible to your shareholders."*
>
> Jim Collins
> USA Today [246]

Ultimately this comes down to fiscal and social responsibility—no,—opportunity!

Let me remind you of how the quality movement got its jumpstart. It was the investment community—combined with daunting offshore competition—that really got the ball rolling for the North American quality movement. When investors heard about the results of the PIMS data on the profit impact of superior quality, they wanted more.[247] And they started *demanding* quality improvements from the organizations they invested in. In turn, taxpayers started demanding the same of their public institutions.

But enlightened leaders were already hopping on the bandwagon. They saw the performance of organizations which excelled at quality, and they wanted a slice of the action.

This is what I would call a pull strategy. Make it *irresistible* for organizations to *want* to pursue this path. In short, cultivate demanding, discriminating stakeholders. And with the dawn of a new millennium, this is the perfect time for us to do the same for health.

There is also a push strategy happening for Balanced Scorecards. The Government Performance and Results Act (GPRA) passed by Congress in 1993 mandated accountability for the U.S. public sector. Not surprisingly, the public sector has been flocking to the Balanced Scorecard as a means to capture balanced performance results. But the spectacular turnarounds in the public sector have whetted the appetite of public sector peers. They want more! So the early successes of the Balanced Scorecard have transformed the push strategy into a pull strategy. This wave is already hitting Canada, even if public sector accountability hasn't yet been legislated.

The predictive Balanced Scorecard offers me the evidence I need to prove that health is not merely a cost centre—it can be a profit centre! For institutional investors already interested in human capital, the Healthy Scorecard offers another layer of impact. It's time to unleash these accountability gorillas[248]— the institutional investors.

GET RICH QUICK!

There is already an exciting body of evidence that healthy leadership boosts stock returns. Here are a few highlights from the research.

The Dollar Value of Human Resources Systems

Preceding the publication of their book, Drs. Becker and Huselid shared their research insights on the "*Best and Worst Human Resources (HR) Systems*" at a Balanced Scorecard Collaborative NetConference.[249] This research, based on four national surveys of over 2,800 firms, focused on the gaps between the bottom 10% of HR Systems, and the top 10%. The key finding of this research was that,

> "(a) 35% improvement in Human Capital Architecture 'quality' (was) linked to a 10-20% gain in shareholder value!"
>
> Becker B., Huselid M.
> The HR Scorecard[250]

Measures that Matter

Recently, Ernst & Young released a report on a groundbreaking study in investment practice. In a report entitled *Measures that Matter*™,[251] the researchers showed that 35% of investors' decisions are driven by nonfinancial factors—the soft side of the organization.

The report cited ten nonfinancial investment criteria that drive valuation decisions:

- Execution of corporate strategy
- Quality of corporate strategy

- Market position
- Management credibility
- Innovativeness
- Management experience
- Research leadership
- Quality of major business processes
- Global capability; and
- Ability to attract and retain talented people.

The kicker to this report is that when investors do consider these soft factors, they make more money! I believe that we can go further: investment performance goes up and risk goes down when we better understand how wellbeing drives human innovation—and hence future growth prospects. In short, health capital is a key driver—maybe *the* key driver—of sustainable growth.

What the Healthy Scorecard and Capability/Wellbeing Index offer then, is a tool for investors to get a better handle on future financial prospects. These tools sharpen our focus upstream, so we can improve our downstream performance.

Watson Wyatt Human Capital Index™

There are many exciting contenders in this race to link human capital with shareholder returns. Watson Wyatt reported on its *Human Capital Index*™—a list of 30 measures, wherein significant improvement drives a 30% increase in shareholder value. These measures are grouped into five high-impact areas:

- Recruiting excellence
- Clear rewards and accountability

➤ A collegial and flexible workplace

➤ Communications integrity; and

➤ Prudent use of resources.[252]

Once again organizational culture, effort/reward, communications quality, and social support come to the fore. Momentum is increasing as investors realize the impact of the soft and fuzzy. And it is ironic that the nebulous "soft side" is giving clarity to the hard-driving investors.[253]

Perhaps it is no surprise that some leading organizations pursuing wellbeing/profitability linkages are being remarkably tight-lipped about their findings. For example, while the Bank of Montreal shares that, *"The bank has found a correlation between a healthy organizational climate and profitability, productivity, customer loyalty and employee turnover"*, their specific findings have been closely guarded to date.[254] If anything, this response should serve as a magnet for investors seeking untapped improvement opportunities.

So is the Healthy Scorecard a get-rich-quick scheme? You tell me.

Cultivating Demanding Stakeholders

Ultimately, I believe the success in mobilizing widespread adoption of a strategic health focus will depend on our success in convincing the investment community that health strategy is not only a *sound* business proposition, but also *irresistible*. Here are a few of the key themes with which we can lure the investment community to this new paradigm:

> *Cultural improvement is a low-hanging fruit.* It adds dramatic value, and reduces costs, most notably health costs, which (Eureka!) we can now measure.

> *Health costs threaten to eclipse profits* –in corporate North America and globally. Period.

> *The do-nothing scenario will only cost you more next year.* And it may put you out of business soon.

> *The Healthy Scorecard is a crystal ball for profits.* It pushes prediction of future financial performance even further upstream. It reduces risk for investors, and increases sustainable returns.

Creating the Climate for Innovation

> *"Does somebody know what it means to 'administer' human imagination? I don't. But I know that imagination is the most important creator of wealth in the New Economy. And I know we had better find the answer to my question—quickly."*
>
> Tom Peters[255]

What does a healthy workplace really buy us? I believe it buys us imagination, which in turn fuels the engine for future financial growth.

I look forward to being able to precisely predict not only how much—but when health and capability improvements will be realized, as a result of implementing a Healthy Scorecard. I look forward to applauding the healthy companies which profit from defying the 2x4 style of management—and have the numbers to prove it! I look forward to the time when health will truly be an irresistible business imperative.

The future is now!

The 5th Perspective: Societal

What really excites me about the Healthy Scorecard and Cost of Health is not just the impact on a single organization, but the potential impact on communities, and entire national health systems. Admittedly this is a future state vision, but perhaps not all that far off. Let me share with you a success story to illustrate my point.

Success Story: The Safe Communities Foundation

The Safe Communities Foundation in Canada has generated some spectacular community safety turnarounds, simply by partnering with stakeholders, providing support, and—perhaps most importantly—holding out a financial carrot to participants. Now while I'd submit that we don't really *need* external inducements to make a business case for health and safety, they do speed things up.

My favorite example is the pilot conducted in High River, Canada, which set the stage for the Safe Communities Foundation. Modelling their approach after the World Health Organization's *Safe Communities* model, the pilot created a partnership with the Worker's Compensation Board of Alberta, Alberta Labour, the High River Chamber of Commerce, and 22 local businesses. They provided top-notch audits and training in injury prevention. They offered direct rebates, negotiated in advance through the Worker's Compensation Board, to organizations for any safety improvements.

And they reduced injuries by a compelling 66% in one year! [256]

Success Vision: From Healthy Workplaces to a Healthier Illness-Care System

Now we need to do the same for health, safety, *and* capability, one community at a time. It is exciting enough to consider the financial impact of the Healthy Scorecard for a single organization.

*But just imagine the impact on entire health regions, provinces, Health Management Organizations, or states, if we could cut our event rates for stress, illness, and injury by at least 50% **en masse**!*

We can do this!

The Vision Takes Shape

At the City of Calgary, Mayor Al Duerr has a vision for an "Ethical City". And Mayor Duerr's vision for an ethical city is just made for this kind of large-scale health strategy.

> *"When we ask Calgarians what issues they consider most important, the most defining answers consistently relate to quality of life issues. I believe there is a direct relationship between a community's ethics and values and its quality of life... I believe it is time for Calgary to subscribe to new indicators of success and measurements that reflect and help us to understand the real, truly important aspects of our quality of life."*[257]

There is a red measure in the City of Calgary Wellness Team's pilot Balanced Scorecard—a measure which we have not yet captured—but which we eventually will. And this is our ability, through our strategic wellbeing initiatives at the City of Calgary (a major employer within the Calgary Regional Health Authority) to reduce the drain on our health care system.

This Societal Perspective in the City's Balanced Scorecard may be linked very shortly with an exciting partnership that is materializing between the Calgary Asthma Program, and the City.

If you recall the Total Cost of Asthma model presented in Chapter 5, we know that we can not only potentially reduce total costs to the City by 30%, but we can also reduce utilization of the stretched community asthma care services. Uncontrolled asthma represents a huge cost to the public health system in the form of emergency room visits and hospitalization. In Edmonton at the Capital Health Authority, pediatric asthma visits alone represent $3 million in hospital costs, and another $7 million in absenteeism costs that are borne by employers when parents are forced to stay home with asthmatic children.

Here is a beautiful example of win to the power of three, when we prevent unnecessary use of the health system:

- *Employees and their dependents win,* with less suffering and better asthma outcomes.

- *The City wins*, with healthier and more productive employees, and lower health costs.

- *The Calgary Asthma Program wins*, with more appropriate utilization of their stretched services, and better capacity to serve others.

Figure 47

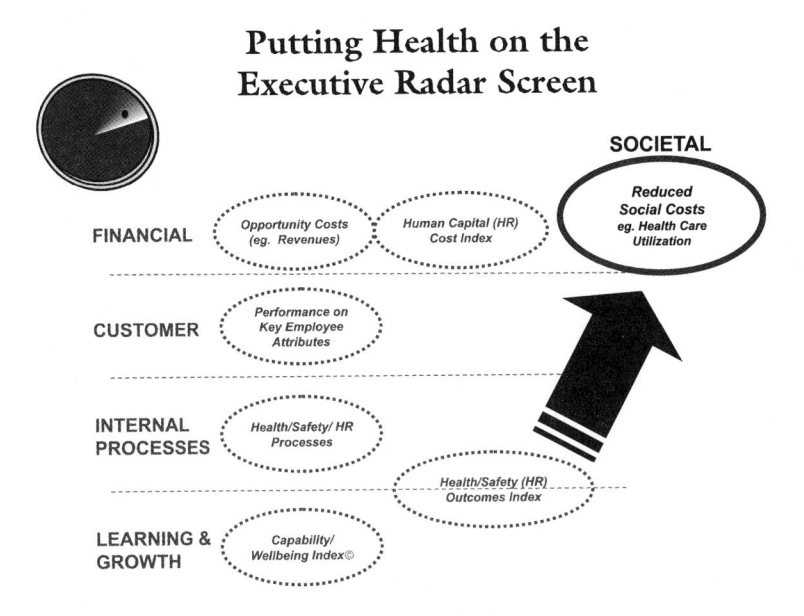

Putting Health on the Executive Radar Screen

FINANCIAL — Opportunity Costs (eg. Revenues) — Human Capital (HR) Cost Index

SOCIETAL — Reduced Social Costs eg. Health Care Utilization

CUSTOMER — Performance on Key Employee Attributes

INTERNAL PROCESSES — Health/Safety/HR Processes

Health/Safety (HR) Outcomes Index

LEARNING & GROWTH — Capability/Wellbeing Index©

Copyright Healthy Business Inc., 2001.

Now all we need is for the Worker's Compensation Board of Alberta, the Calgary Regional Health Authority, and Alberta Health to put their heads together to concoct a financial carrot for the City—and other employers—to want to do this *today*. And we can measure this in the scorecard for the City, as well as for the Calgary Regional Health Authority. (Fig. 47)

Just imagine the impact on our health system—not to mention our national productivity—if we could mobilize entire communities to improve health and capability!

A Canadian Approach

In Canada, this vision could be kick-started by orchestrating a funding formula—certainly not the current *use-it-or-lose-it* approach—which would reinvest dollars to successful employers. Ideally this would also return some of the benefits into the health system.

If there is any principle of Canadian Medicare that is already slipping, it is that of *comprehensiveness*.[258] Regional Health Authorities (RHA's) could direct some of the dollar savings as an incentive to workplaces to reduce stress, illness, and injury. But the RHA's could also reinvest some of the savings into a discretionary health spending account for the community. This money could be directed into high-need areas, or to enhancements to the comprehensiveness of care. In this way, entire communities might be motivated to make their neighborhood a "*best place to live*".

Many communities should become motivated to do this. After all, quality of life is going to become increasingly linked to the success of an economic region in attracting and retaining a talented workforce.

Let me give you an example of why this is so very timely. The Government of Alberta recently awarded a $300 million contract for network investment to the Bell consortium. Flush with cash, the province of Alberta wants to become the Silicon Valley of the North—and is investing aggressively to build a high-speed Internet infrastructure, clear across the province.

> "...the project is part of a government strategy that envisions Information and Communications Technology as a means to improve the quality of life and build sustainable prosperity for Albertans."
>
> Bell Canada Media Relations
> *Government of Alberta awards $300 million network investment to Bell* [259]

But is it enough to develop just the *physical* infrastructure for such an ambitious project? Or do we also need to develop the *human capital* infrastructure and leadership capability, so that we can populate these new business opportunities with talent? Because this dynamic initiative is occurring against the backdrop of a country facing a critical shortage of 1 million skilled workers! (*Skilled worker shortage could reach one million*, Globe and Mail cover story, February 27, 2001.) This is the War for Talent on a huge scale! So I'm throwing down the gauntlet for entire regions, such as the Province of Alberta to act on this human capital challenge.

A U.S. Approach

> *"The light is dawning at forward- thinking managed care organizations like Humana and United Healthcare, that employers might pay them more for higher-value outcomes, such as lower total health costs, and improved employee functionality."*
>
> Sean Sullivan, President and CEO,
> Institute for Health and Productivity Management[260]

Large-scale community mobilization could work in the United States as well—or in any country for that matter. Any Health Management Organization or private insurer worth its salt will recognize that improved clinical outcomes represent value-add that customers will pay for. And preventing event rates in the first place is the ultimate clinical outcome.

Now why not accelerate this process by providing short-term financial inducements?

The Future: Intersecting Balanced Scorecards

What we are ultimately talking about is what makes society tick—how organizational Balanced Scorecards *intersect*. In other words, we are mapping out the win/win between different organizations in society. And if the various stakeholders have a Balanced Scorecard, the win/win is explicitly spelled out.

<u>Linking Employers with the Health System</u>

For example the City of Calgary's Societal measure of reducing the drain on the health care system is intuitively shared by Calgary Asthma Program's objective to improve clinical outcomes, and to optimize effective use of their limited resources. And these are shared with the Worker's Compensation Board's vision of "*Albertans Working: A Safe, Healthy, and Strong Alberta.*"[261]

Intersecting Balanced Scorecards map out the roles and synergy of players in a larger network. And they have powerful implications for the health system. For example, in consulting to the Worker's Safety and Insurance Board (WSIB) of Ontario with Jim Clemmer a few of years ago, it was clear to us that measurement and alignment were two sides of the same coin.

Ontario has 14 Safe Work Associations—some with overlapping mandates—which rely on the support of the Ministry of Labour's enforcement function, as well as the WSIB's audit and financial incentive role, to improve safety results. Simply having a Safe Work Association train an employee in chainsaw safety will not reduce injuries if the employee is working in an environment where throughput is king. Managers in workplaces need to be aware—through a combination of carrots (through the Healthy Scorecard and possible WCB rebates) and sticks, (in the forms of Ministry of Labour enforcement, or WCB penalties)—that safety does indeed pay.

Linking Health and Safety

Intersecting Balanced Scorecards are a good thing. They break down the silos and highlight the crossovers between health and safety; occupational and nonoccupational risk management, and mental and physical health.

The Crossover: Health and Safety

For example a truck driver with migraines poses a substantial safety risk. Migraines don't only make you feel badly, they can obliterate your peripheral vision—a daunting prospect when you're driving an eighteen-wheeler.[262] So effective migraine management is integral to safety improvement.

But we shouldn't stop there. Because migraines are frequently triggered by stress and lack of sleep.[263] And sleep deprivation in turn bleeds reaction times. This brings up the prospect that work organization, work/life initiatives, and enlightened shift structures are also part of the picture of improving truck safety.

And this gives rise to my prediction that the Balanced Scorecard for Worker's Compensation Boards will—and should intersect with objectives for private insurers, migraine clinics, work/life initiatives, and sleep clinics—in short, the health and human resources systems. High time too!

As we enter the New Economy, we also need to be aware of the crossover between occupational and nonoccupational illness and injury. For example, is it a work-related injury if you have a car accident while couriering a package to a client? How about if you drop off your children at school, on your way to a business meeting? As more people telecommute, the distinction between work and non-related work risk is becoming blurred, if not irrelevant. Self-interested workplaces *need* to keep employees healthy!

Closing

The Strategic Gap

Most organizations still delegate health and safety to technical professionals. Fact is, most managers are unaware of the mountain of evidence that leadership has everything to do with superior health and safety results. And this lack of awareness prevents us from capturing the powerful upstream drivers of stress, illness, and injury—not to mention the drivers of innovation, resilience, and vigorous financial performance.

Even when workplaces recognize the health/leadership linkage, many do not provide the necessary management rigor to "lock in" health and safety values... through robust measures, accountabilities, and systems.

At the same time, there is a War for Talent, and a major strategic gap which prevents organizations from achieving meaningful business results. Yet execution of corporate strategy is central to our success. What's holding us back? Dr. Kaplan, co-author of *The Balanced Scorecard* recently shared the following key challenges to strategic implementation:

> - **"Vision**: Only 5% of the workforce understands the strategy
> - **People:** 75% of organizations do not link managers' incentives to strategy
> - **Resources:** 60% of organizations do not link budgets to strategy; and
> - **Reporting:** 92% of organizations do not report on lead indicators."

Dr. Robert Kaplan,
The Balanced Scorecard[264]

Not surprisingly, the biggest gap in strategy is in addressing the "soft" side of the organization—people. And as Dr. Kaplan rightly notes, the Healthy Scorecard is, *"addressing the softest aspects of the employee measurement system, which in itself is about the softest of the BSC measures!"*[265] I see this as an exciting opportunity. For even in the field of human capital management, employee wellbeing remains largely marginalized. Yet, as we have learned, robust predictive linkages can be made between soft employee attitudes, employee capability and wellbeing, and hard financial results.

The successful execution of organizational strategy is as important to employees as it is to executives and investors. In fact, I would offer that strategic alignment is one of the most powerful health enhancers available.

I am reminded of a clip from *"I Love Lucy"*, when Lucille Ball took a job at a chocolate factory. It was her job to wrap chocolates going by on a conveyor belt. And as the conveyor belt accelerated past her abilities, she started frantically stuffing them in her pockets and her mouth. This is a classic example of strategic misalignment—where the wrong individual is poorly trained to do a job for which the processes are not in good working order, and where the perceived goal (speed) is at odds with the organization's needs (quality). Hiding the chocolates does nothing to improve the bottom line—for Lucy or for the company.

By providing a line of sight for individual employees to organizational strategy, the Balanced Scorecard imbues our work with meaning. The BSC also supports work/life balance, since it forces us to identify, "*What will we not do?*".

Good Health is Good Accounting is Great Business

For too long, we have indulged sloppy accounting practices which miss not just the boat, but also the engine of wellbeing and high performance: leadership. If you get what you measure, the Healthy Scorecard puts us on the road to superior performance. The captivating reality is that in measuring and addressing leading indicators for health and high performance, we can have our cake and eat it too! Cheap, but not easy, for this requires that we ask the tough questions, from the front line to the executive office, on how *well* we're doing.

From Measurement to Renewal

> "*Good, balanced measures on a Healthy Scorecard don't give you the answers but rather they prompt you to ask better questions that drive you to root cause problem solving and process improvement that are the answers.*"
>
> Mark Henderson
> Executive Vice President, The Clemmer Group

I am indebted to my colleague Mark Henderson for underscoring the importance of the *process* of the Healthy Scorecard, rather than merely the metrics.[266] Let me emphasize that for the Healthy Scorecard to succeed, it must be used as a *process* for continual renewal and alignment, not as a static measurement tool. I submit that there is a capitalistic—and existential—pleasure in seeing these causal relationships between leadership, employee wellbeing/capability, and the bottom line play out. It's the ultimate win/win.

The And/And Solution

But let's come back down to earth for a moment. What the Healthy Scorecard offers is not a panacea for all ills, but a lubricant to supercharge your performance engine. As my esteemed colleague Owen Griffiths would say, "*It's not enough to have delighted employees…. you must **also** be aligned to your market, customers, and processes.*"[267] And you must excel at your strategic execution.

This is where I see the gap—and the opportunity—in the Balanced Scorecard.

Strategic execution will never be optimized until we harness the universal drivers of superior and sustained human performance: employee wellbeing and capability.

Our renewed understanding of the capability/wellbeing synergy cuts across all boundaries—it's the essence of being human, and the key driver of *sustained* organizational success.

The challenge I pose, is for us to implement this newfound knowledge in our *corporate* balanced scorecards: simply, clearly, frequently, and consistently.

It's time to do for employee wellbeing what we know how to do for service/quality excellence. If quality can be free, health can be too! Let's stop rearranging the deck chairs on the Titanic, and start plugging some holes. Better yet, let's avoid the icebergs in the first place!

*Good health is good leadership
is great business... and now,
thanks to the Balanced Scorecard,
we can prove it!*

LEADERSHIP CHECK-UP

Investor Issues

1) On what information do you base your current investment decisions?
2) How confident are you in your ability to predict future financial performance?
3) In the absence of healthy, motivated employees:

    a) Is strategic execution sustainable?

    b) Can enduring value be created?
4) What are the implications for your investment decisions? For the investment community?

Thriving on Innovation

5) Are you fighting the War for Talent?

    *a) How **well** are your employees?*
6) Are you wired for innovation?

    *a) How **well** are your employees?*

    b) Does your Balanced Scorecard capture the basic drivers of wellbeing and capability, as well as strategic HR capabilities?
7) Does your measurement system serve as a static tool, or as a vital learning, action, and renewal loop?

Leadership Legacy

8) What are you doing to leave a healthy leadership legacy for your organization?

Further Reading

Acknowledgements

One of the joys of being an entrepreneur is that I can do what I want with my intellectual property. This book is the product of my impatience with the carnage we are wreaking on the health of our organizations... and my enthusiastic impatience for a quantum leap for health *and* high performance. Now that I can finally help organizations to capture the opportunity costs of health, I'm brimming with excitement about this spectacular new frontier! I hope to share with you the sources of my frustration, as well as the data to support my unbridled optimism.

Oscar Wilde once said, "*True friends stab you in the front.*" There is perhaps no better time to be stabbed in the front than when you are editing a book. I have been supported to write this book long before I actually put pen to paper. This work gives me the opportunity to say, "Thank you" to the many people who have supported me in pursuing this vision. You know who you are.

There is a posse of supporters to whom I owe a massive debt of gratitude. These renegades include Canada's Health Strategy Team at Glaxo Wellcome, most notably Ken Boutilier for his courage and conviction in sticking his neck out for me, and his unwavering vision, support, integrity, and tenacity to see this book come to fruition. Also Lise Jantzon for her uncanny understanding of health strategy, her deeply ingrained human values, her awe-inspiring command of *Health Evidence's* capabilities, and her wisdom and candor in critiquing this book; Dan Clow for not wanting his plane to land while he was reading an early version of the manuscript, for his four versions of, "*For now we see through a glass, darkly*", and for his enthusiastic, discreet, and incisive contributions; and the backdrop of Health Strategy Team members who went out on a limb repeatedly to support this project. Thank you.

I am also indebted to Health Canada and the Centre for Addiction and Mental Health for their sponsorship of this project, and to Terrence Dalton, André Nolet, and Martin Shain for their generous mentoring. Martin's grace, brilliance, organizational health innovations, and intellectual generosity have blazed a path for followers in this field, and we are all indebted to him. To Terrence Dalton, I extend my thanks for keeping Healthy Business Inc. afloat—intellectually and economically—with fascinating work in the early years, and encouragement throughout.

Writing this book was a little like growing crystals in science class. It started off with tiny seeds that proved invaluable in helping me wrap my head around health, rehabilitation, leadership, quality, performance measurement, strategy, and high performance. To Kathy Obright, physiotherapist extraordinaire, I extend my deep thanks for supporting and affirming my decision to forge a career in health and business; to Professor Tony Dimnik, academic and practical enthusiast at the Ivey Business School, my sincere appreciation for encouraging me to research the business case for healthy workplaces; to my peers at the Ivey Business School in the early 90's, my thanks for leaning forward in your seats when I shared that corporate health costs in the U.S. exceed net after-tax profits. And to Tony de Castro, I extend my gratitude for giving me my first

Further Reading

organizational health contract—and a marvelous learning opportunity as an entrepreneur.

When this book was in its infancy, many people were instrumental in adding fuel to my fire. My sincere thanks to Dr. Jim Stewart for sharing his extraordinary understanding of world class safety, and for indulging and challenging—and thus stretching—my systems approach to employee wellbeing. Many thanks also to Ralph McGinn and Bart Jessup from the Worker's Compensation Board of B.C., Nan Bennett of the Healthcare Benefit Trust; Bryan Lowes of the B.C. Safety Council; and Jim Stimson of MacMillan Bloedel (now Weyerhaeuser) for encouraging me to undertake this work. Also my thanks to Ken Isomura of the United Way Labour Participation Department, who helped me learn about labour, as well as business perspectives on health; Bill Blundell for his encouragement to write about empowerment as a driver of health; Paul Haggis and Ted Pattenden for being an occasional executive sounding board; Charlie Black for molding my early vision for wide-scale prevention; Larry Green for dissuading me from doing a PhD, and urging me to "*Just do it*", in the hands-on world of business; and Sue Hills health promotion pioneer and founder of the Alliance for Health and Fitness, whose early encouragement, mentorship, passion for win/win strategies, and friendship spurred me to pursue a career in a (virtually) nonexistent field.

My sincere appreciation also to Dianne Dyck for taking me under her wing, and introducing me to the City of Calgary; to Pam Meunier for rekindling my relationship with the City... and a special thanks to Martin Law for his courage, capability and passion for working on this bleeding edge; and David Watson, Deb Mayberry, Dave Denoon, Neil McKendrick, and John Hubbell at the City of Calgary for creating such spectacular learning and growth opportunities. It has been a fascinating learning experience.

There are a number of other leaders in this field to whom I

am deeply grateful for learning opportunities over the years. These include Tom Carson, Julian Barling, Wayne Corneil, Terrence Sullivan, Lynda Robson, Doug Cowan, Nora Spinks, Linda Duxbury, and Tony Roithmayr.

There are also a number of "rain men" who have contributed strategic opportunities for me to push the envelope. These include Sean Sullivan, Kent Peterson, Raven Ruffner, and Michael Moriarity of the Institute for Health and Productivity Management; Judy MacBride-King and Kim Bachmann of the Conference Board of Canada; Evan Perkins of The Gallup Organization; Deb Jones of the Health Work and Wellness Conference; Terrence Sullivan and Lynda Robson of the Institute for Work and Health; John Charette of the Manitoba Federal Council; Marianne Levitsky of the Worker's Safety and Insurance Board; Maureen Shaw of the Industrial Accident Prevention Association; Elizabeth Mills of the Ontario Service Safety Alliance; Tom MacLeod of the Industrial, Wood & Allied Workers of Canada – Forest Industry and Long Term Disability Plan; and Marlene Ruddell of the Canadian Human Resources Planners. Among this group of rain men are the many researchers and organizations—referenced in the Notes section—that generously gave me permission to cite their work. Thank you.

The real turning point for my work came when I stumbled across the *Harvard Business Review* article on the *Employee-Customer-Profit Chain at Sears*, and research on the Service Profit Chain and Balanced Scorecard. Thanks to a snowstorm in Washington, I was able to make the acquaintance of Dr. Bob Kaplan, who has been a gracious and patient sounding board for my musings on bottom-up ballast for the top-down Balanced Scorecard. I would also like to make special mention of Lauren St. John, health promotion luminary, whose vision, integrity, courage, and excellence in organizational health rocketed my experience curve. Thank you.

There are two spikes in my recent learning curve, which have rocketed my ability to address this synergy between health and high performance. These include my tenure with the Clemmer Group, and my learning from the International Quality and Productivity Centre. My sincere thanks to my former Clemmer Group colleagues Jim and Heather Clemmer for including me in the Clemmer Group fold; to Mark Henderson for introducing me to the Balanced Scorecard and for his continuing intellectual generosity; and Tom Gallagher and "digital diva" Julie Gil for their warm and enthusiastic support. Special thanks also to Owen Griffiths for his authenticity, his unwavering enthusiasm for the health/quality linkage from the get-go, and for his honesty in pushing me to make this work appealing to executives. Also I owe awe and gratitude to Merle Dulmadge, my coach, mentor, and friend, for an unending source of laughter, wisdom, and red ink. Thank you for reminding me that windows of opportunity can open—and close.

If you get what you pay for, the International Quality and Productivity Centre (IQPC) over-delivers! Many thanks to Laura Coy and Elizabeth Mayo for creating such spectacular learning and sharing experiences, and to the many leading presenters at the intimate Balanced Scorecard for Government 2000 conference, and the spectacular HR Measurement 2000 and 2001 conferences, which have leap-frogged my systems approach to health.

There is nothing like nepotism to help a project, and I am happy to say that I benefited richly from it. When your father is a linguist, your mother is a writer, and your sister is a devotee of English literature and Greek mythology, you can't help but grow up with a love for language and literature. It was a no-brainer to turn to Dr. Geoffrey O'Grady and Alix O'Grady, both "Boundary Riders" extraordinaire and my lifetime mentors, for editorial advice. It has been my privilege to walk in the shadow of these giants.

And when your 18 year old nephew is a website hot-dog, it is only logical to make him your Webmaster. Many thanks to Aaron Deacon and his supportive family for getting my work out there on the Net.

Patronage works too, so many, many thanks to my Ivey friends Katherine Brown and Asiff Hirji for their sage and oft-humorous advice, and to Sherri Lupton and Darlene Firth for their eagle-eyed editing excellence.

When it comes to editing books, I am a Luddite, and no one knows this better than my typesetter extraordinaire, Roy Diment of Vivencia Resources Group. As we reached the "final" edits for this book, the light kept getting brighter at the end of the tunnel… but the tunnel kept getting longer. Roy's patience, expertise, and can-do attitude were a saving grace, and he has indeed been a joy to work with. I am also delighted to sing the praises of Trafford Publishing, notably Bruce Batchelor, Publisher and CEO, for his let-me-make-it-easy-for-you approach to publishing, and his state-of-the-art "On Demand" publishing capabilities; and Sarah Campbell, Author Services Representative, for her professionalism and gentle efficiency in keeping my publishing priorities straight. Thank you also to Jim Overland at PostNet for his spectacular efficiency in couriering wave after wave of manuscripts to reviewers. And as many readers will recognize, I also owe credit to my favorite source of clipart—Microsoft. Except where otherwise indicated, all clipart is obtained from Microsoft Clip Gallery.

Starting a business or writing a book in an empty field is no small feat, and I was afforded the uncommon luxury of total intellectual freedom to pursue my vision, by my husband and best friend, Tim. Aside from never saying, *"Show me the money"*, he provided mentorship, balance, fun, and love—not a bad way to run a small business. Standing by for moral support during the writing of this book was also a gaggle of extraordinary friends who have stood by me through the years, and who never urged me to sell out and get a "real" job. My thanks to

Lynelle Phillips and Carolyn Kroeber for their uncanny blend of professional advice, quirky wisdom, and warm comic relief; to Suromitra Sanatani for our 20 years of synergy, feedback, and growth; and to Iolanda Millar, friend, editor, humorist, and mentor for me in these murky waters of the publishing world.

One of the blessings in my life is that I have two small but powerful VP's who share my workplace. As my own boss, I have decided how much I want to work, and full-time is not in the picture. But on the days I work in my home office, I rely on the loving support of our friends and caregivers, Sherri Lupton and Cathie Craib, and the assistance of industrial earplugs. My deepest thanks to all of you!

Finally, I would like to thank the reader for indulging my strong biases in this field. Those who know me well know that it was a Herculean task for me to try to be subtle. This is such a captivating—and shockingly empty—field, that I yielded to the advice of Winston Churchill:

"If you have an important point to make, don't try to be subtle or clever. Use a pile driver. Hit the point once. Then come back and hit it again. Then hit it a third time— a tremendous whack."

Many thanks for your patience as I did just that!

PUTTING MORE HEALTH MYTHS TO REST

In this section, I continue debunking health myths, which I began in Chapter 2. I have removed these final myths from the body of the text to allow readers to sink their teeth more quickly into the data of Chapters 3 and beyond. For myths #1-4, please revisit Chapter 2: *Redefining Health and the Balanced Scorecard*.

<u>Myth #5: Continuous Improvement is a Good Thing</u>

"Something is rotten in the State of Denmark."

William Shakespeare,
Hamlet, Act 1, Scene 4

Our infatuation with continuous improvement is one of the most destructive forces eroding organization improvement. The general idea is that as long as you're better this year or this quarter than the last one, then you're succeeding. And you can relax.

Fact:

Unfortunately, this couldn't be farther from the truth:

*Continuous improvement
is the road to mediocrity!*

As the average organizations putter forward with marginal improvements, a handful of extraordinary organizations are redefining standards of excellence in health, safety, and organizational performance.

*What has largely escaped the attention
of the business community is the
chasm in health and safety outcomes
between the average and stellar organizations*

Dr. Jim Stewart, a renowned Canadian safety maverick recently completed a review of some of the world's best safety performers, and found that their safety performance was in the order of **100 times** better than the average performer![23]

C. Milliken & Company is one company which is relentlessly pursuing a world-class safety record. Milliken's average Total Recordable Injury Frequency was 0.88 between 1993 and 1997, which was 8.5 times better than the U.S. Textile sector. In other words, for every two employees injured at Milliken, 17 are injured at industry counterparts. Milliken is a key customer of Dupont, noted for its world-class safety record. Thanks to a dedicated focus on excellence in everything they do, Milliken is now threatening to eclipse the performance of safety giants such as Dupont.[24]

There is a similar chasm for health results. Stress-related illness—a scourge of the New Economy—is almost a non-issue in a handful of extraordinarily enlightened companies. Yet under the patina of continuous improvement, most organizations are blissfully committing to mediocre performance.

Myth #6: Industry Comparisons Spur Improvement

Red lights go on for me when a client enthuses that their health and safety performance, or their employee retention rate, is better than that of their competitors. And warning bells blare when they comfortably state, *"We're right where we should be—at the average for our industry"*. The idea is that we should feel comforted that our organization is running at the speed of the pack.

Fact:

> *"Visionary companies focus primarily on beating themselves."*
>
> James C. Collins, Jerry I. Porras
> Built to Last

In this context of a War for Talent, the pursuit of world-class health, safety, and business results depends on creating a burning platform for change. Being marginally better than your immediate competitors is small consolation when you could be a hundred times better!

Industry comparisons reinforce complacency

Used in isolation, industry comparisons merely reinforce complacency with the current state, and corrode our attempts to leverage human capital. Industry comparisons are particularly dangerous, as in the case of employee wellbeing, when the gap between world class and average is wide.

Interestingly, Dr. Jim Stewart found in his research on world-class safety that the best performers were deeply *dissatisfied* with their performance![25] This constructive dissatisfaction is a good thing, and is *necessary* to drive superior performance!

Industry comparisons stifle the vision for a future state

In "*Built to Last*", James Collins and Jerry Porras write about the importance of "BHAGs", or *Big, Hairy, Audacious Goals* in transforming organizational performance. Benchmarking performance against industry norms ensures that any definition of the Future State will never be a BHAG[26].

Due to the crippling awareness gap of the huge improvement potential in workplace health, BHAGs related to employee wellbeing are virtually unheard-of!

But not for long! For there is an abundance of research data which demonstrates that leaders have *everything* to do with superior results. A major paradigm shift is required for us to see wellbeing as a core leadership issue.

Can we turn this ship around?

> *"For now we see through a glass, darkly;*
> *but then face to face...."*
>
> 1 Corinthians, 13:9-13
> *King James Version Bible*

I have spoken about the awareness barrier which prevents us from pursuing BHAGS in employee wellbeing. In my view, this is the greatest barrier to sustaining high performance. For we already possess the skills to turn around organizational culture, to lead people and manage organizations more effectively, to align improvement efforts with robust management systems, and to apply strategic measurement and management systems. Now we must link these skills with employee health.

Linking health with corporate strategy is cheap, highly profitable, and in many ways, easy! As Ted Pattenden, CEO of National Rubber Inc., commented on his ten-fold turnaround in lost time injuries, [27]

> *"This was not an issue of throwing money at (health and safety), this was an issue of throwing management intensity at it."*

Payday

A vital condition for substantive change in health and safety results is that managers view the change initiative as worth the effort. There must be a perceived payoff. I hope to convince you that the payoff for employee wellbeing is not only substantial, but also exciting!

A few years ago, a senior Human Resources executive for a major resource-based corporation cheerfully told me,

> "Frankly, we're pleased when we improve our safety record one year, and then are able to sit back for a while."

This executive clearly hadn't done the math. Shown in the top bar in Figure 2, this company's improvement track stands in sharp contrast to the rapid turnaround of NRI Industries Inc.,[28] reflected in the bottom bar, or the sustained improvements of world-class organizations such as Dupont Canada, shown in the middle bar, which reduce their injury rate by 30% *per year*.[29] Most importantly, this executive wasn't counting opportunity costs.

Figure 2

What does your improvement track look like?

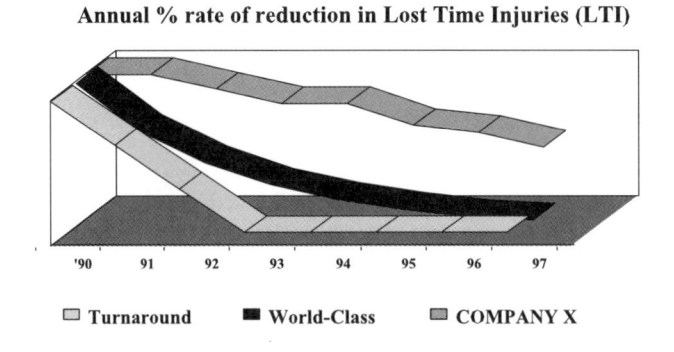

Annual % rate of reduction in Lost Time Injuries (LTI)

☐ Turnaround ■ World-Class ☐ COMPANY X

Source: Company X Annual Report 1997, Personal communication, Dr. Jim Stewart; personal communication, Ted Pattenden, CEO, NRI, at Industrial Accident Prevention Association Conference, Toronto, 1998.

The payoff for superior health and safety is not just in risk management for spectacular incidents. In fact, I submit that there is a silent epidemic of Exxon Valdez disasters... not the highly publicized disasters, but the unspectacular yet relentless occurrence of stress, illness, and injury in ordinary workplaces, which corrodes our life and our competitive performance.

And while massive environmental destruction has proven to be an effective way to focus attention on health and safety, there is another way. The Healthy Scorecard provides us a tool to capture not only spectacular *cost hits*, but more importantly the insidious but profound *value lost* when our workforce is stressed, ill, or injured. Most important, the Healthy Scorecard is a *process* to drive root cause analysis and action further upstream. It is this process, not the metrics *per se*, which drives sustainable high performance.[30]

Myth #7: For Best Results, Delegate Health to Experts

As our world becomes more sophisticated, we are lured by the sexy notion that specialists are the best ones to deal with our problems. This myth is alive and well when it comes to health and safety, and legions of managers blissfully delegate health issues to technical professionals.

The misguided notion is that, "Health is not a management issue ... leave it to the experts".

Fact:

> *Managers have no idea they are part of the equation (to improve health). In fact, they **are** the equation!*
>
> Martin Law,
> City of Calgary[31]

In fairness to the health profession, many practitioners are unfamiliar with the latest research on how leadership factors impact health and safety outcomes. Others are acting in misguided protection of their turf. While I write as a former rehabilitation specialist, having worked both as an Occupational Therapist and Industrial Physiotherapist, I still believe that it is dangerous for health professionals to position themselves as turnkey experts in workplace health, or for leaders to delegate health away from the corner office.

I left Physiotherapy and Occupational Therapy—both professions which guarantee cash for life—frustrated that there was no way that we alone could meet the escalating demand for our services. If anything, it should come as a massive relief to many health care providers that we can stem the bleeding—and prevent many employees from needing health services in the first place.

Myth #8: Your Health Issues are Unique

> *"Always remember you're unique, just like everyone else."*
>
> Bumper Sticker

It is easy to be seduced by the notion that each workplace has unique employee health issues. After all, employee demographics and work environments vary wildly, even within a given organization.

But this book focuses on what leaders can do to deliver enduring and superior business results. And the danger in this myth is that we lose sight of the proverbial forest for the trees.

Fact:

When it comes right down to it, the leadership drivers of health are universal. In fact, if your workplace doesn't have the basics of fairness, trust, respect, purpose, and excellent communication, you are guaranteed to have problems with employee health and safety, not to mention with your strategic execution.

Revisit Chapter 6, where I commit consulting and research heresy, by going down the "one-size-fits-all" path, to outline a *Capability/Wellbeing Index*©: a deliciously simple and concise process which can be used quarterly to predict your organizational and financial health. This index is akin to a hierarchy of needs, which captures the primeval motivators of employee capability and wellbeing... something the vast majority of organizations are not (yet) doing.

Myth #9: Everyone Values Health

I have yet to find a group of leaders who do not value employee wellbeing. Most leaders truly think they value health. But passively valuing health is a different story from actively influencing it, or living it.

The vast majority of managers believe they have no influence over employee stress, illness, and injury rates.

This makes it easy to value health. After all, accidents happen, and people just get sick, don't they?

Fact:

It is impossible for us to truly value something unless we can demonstrate our commitment by doing something to protect it. As long as managers feel that they are passive bystanders to stress, illness, and injury, it is easy to be seduced into "valuing" health. And we are then tempted to treat health as a fixed cost, rather than something which we can control.

But if you do a diligent enough job in the accounting department, and capture not only the Good and the Bad health costs, but also the Ugly opportunity costs (see Chapter 5 for the *Full Monty* Cost of Health Model), you will be compelled to position employee wellbeing as a core organizational value on mere economic grounds, if not also human grounds. And you will find your focus shifting from cost containment to strategic investment in health.

In fact, I submit it's unethical for us NOT to put health in economic terms, because the *nexgen* business case is so compelling. Map out the cause-and-effect of health in a Strategy Map[32]—as we did in Chapter 6, and you build executive excitement for breakthrough results.

Giving Teeth to our Health Values

Once we have overcome this awareness barrier, we need to give teeth to our health values. And this boils down to one word: accountability.

But we must not only demand accountability for results, we must also build capability—in the form of leadership bench strength—for healthy leadership. And we must build understanding and trust that it is *fair* to hold our managers accountable for these results.

The Healthy Scorecard brings choice into the equation by convincing managers—through the optics of a Strategy Map[33]—that they *can* make a huge difference in health, in a way which benefits employees and business results.

> *"Choosing to be held accountable for results is different than being held accountable."*
>
> Peter Block
> *The Empowered Manager*[34]

The Healthy Scorecard gives teeth to our health values. It puts employee wellbeing on the *corporate* scorecard and empirically validates our continuing investment in health capital.

Myth #10: It is Good to Nail down Responsibilities for Health/Safety

Much rhetoric has been invested in the contentious debate over, *"Whose responsibility is employee wellbeing?"* Popular wisdom suggests that it is useful to nail down responsibilities for health/safety. At one extreme, employees are exhorted to lead risk-free (and might I add, rather boring) lives of Spartan purity. And on the other hand, managers are fingered as agents of the Underworld, and the cause of all ills.

But before jumping into this quagmire, let's take a deep breath… and abandon this silly rhetoric.

Nailing down "responsibilities"—while appealing in a fundamental kind of way—will only poison your workplace culture—and in doing so, will drive up your stress, illness, and injury rates.

Fact:

More to the point is the deeper issue of, *"Who has the opportunity to influence—and benefit from—employee wellbeing?"* In a nutshell, *"What works best?"* The responsibility rhetoric only inflames passions—it doesn't get the job done.

The Time Factor

Consider the example of a single parent, who is time-stressed, overweight and out of shape. Let's say this is a single mom, with 3 kids and a full-time job. Simply telling this woman to exercise isn't going to cut it. Chances are, she wants to feel healthier. What this woman needs is *time*. In fact, in a national survey of employee health needs, Health Canada found that the biggest barrier to Canadians pursuing health interests was time.[35]

The Department of National Defence (DND) in Canada took an innovative approach to the time crunch in the 1980's by making it *convenient* for employees to exercise. In many divisions of DND, employees were encouraged: "*If you choose to exercise at lunch, take 1 ½ hrs. If you choose not to, take your *regular hour.*"[36] This kind of enlightened approach gets at the root of the problem, and makes it easier for employees to improve their own health.

Doing What Works – Smoking Cessation

We run into a similar challenge with smoking cessation. The Conference Board of Canada produced statistics that show that employees who smoke, cost their workplaces on average $2565/year more in incremental health costs and absenteeism, than their non-smoking counterparts.[37] Not surprisingly, employers want them to butt out, but many lack the policies and practices in place to support this enormously difficult task.

And it's a cop-out for workplaces to simply tell employees to stop. Nicotine is a drug which is more addictive than cocaine. And on average a smoker fails 5-7 times, before they succeed.[38] So what smoking employees need is understanding, a lot of patience, professional support for behavior modification, and an environment which *continually* makes it easy for them to quit.

It is this *culture of convenience* which makes the most difference in health promotion. Far from being paternalistic, this just makes good health and business sense.

> *"Valuing employees means committing to their satisfaction, development, and wellbeing.*
>
> *Increasingly, this involves more flexible, high performance work practices, tailored to employees with diverse workplace and home-life needs."*
>
> Baldridge National Quality Program 2001
> *Criteria for Performance Excellence*[39]

I was once challenged by a senior executive of a Canadian hospital who commented: *"It's not my job to keep my employees happy. Life is tough. They should deal with it."*

My response remains: *"You're absolutely right. But it IS your job to deliver superior customer service. And you can't possibly do that if your employees are stressed[40], ill, or injured."*

Like it or not, organizations are in the business of employee wellbeing.

For now we've learned that organizational culture: 360° communication, meaningful empowerment, and work/life balance, have as much—if not more—to do with employee wellbeing, than treadmills and carrot sticks! Threatening news for those of us entrenched in a medical model of health.

If we are truly interested in reducing employee health costs, it makes no sense to exhort employees to exercise regularly, yet still provide them with unsafe workstations or a toxic cultural environment. We are missing the point if we leave it all up to employees.

In the end, the responsibility rhetoric is the most destructive thing that has happened to organizational health efforts. Let's get rid of this baby once and for all, and focus on partnerships.

NOTES

CHAPTER 1:
THE UNTAPPED FRONTIER

[1] Rucci A.J., Kirn S.P., Quinn R.T. The Employee-Customer-Profit Chain at Sears. *Harvard Business Review*, January/February 1998, pp. 83-97.

[2] Dr. Robert S. Kaplan, Marvin Bower Professor of Leadership Development. *The Balanced Scorecard*. Presentation to Balanced Scorecard for Government 2000 Conference, International Quality & Productivity Centre, Washington D.C., January, 2000. Dr. Kaplan emphatically does not endorse measuring what we have. As he commented in a recent note to the author, *"Avoid the syndrome of wanting what you can measure, when you can't measure what you want."*

[3] Ken Webb, Manager, Corporate Safety and Health, B.C. Hydro. *The Development of a Health Report*. Presentation to Health Work and Wellness Conference 2000, Toronto. For more information on the B.C. Hydro Health Report, visit www.bchydro.bc.ca .

[4] Personal communication, Tom Mercyk, Strategic Management Team, City of Calgary, April 2000.

[5] Personal communication, Lieutenant-Colonel David A. Wrather, Deputy Project Director, PMO - Quality of Life, National Defence Headquarters, May 2000.

[6] Rucci A.J., Kirn S.P., Quinn R.T. *Op. cit.*

[7] RBI: Baseball term for Runs Batted In.

Chapter 2:
Redefining the Balanced Scorecard

[8] The Balanced Scorecard is hailed by Harvard Business Review as *"the most influential management idea in the past 75 years"*. *Harvard Business Review*, as cited by the Press Release Network, www.pressreleasenetwork.com .

[9] Kaplan R.S., Norton D.P. Having Trouble with your Strategy? Then Map it! *Harvard Business Review*, September/October 2000, pp. 167 – 176.

[10] Press Release Network, *Op. Cit.*

[11] Kaplan R., Norton D., Having Trouble with your Strategy? Then Map It. *Op. cit.*

[12] Personal communication, Dr. Robert Kaplan, December 2000.

[13] We'll explore these psychological and social (psychosocial) drivers of wellbeing and capability in Chapter 4.

[14] At the 2000 BSC for Government conference, Dr. Kaplan agreed that Sears Roebuck & Co. has the most robust predictive scorecard in the world to date. See Chapter 6 for more on the Sears Roebuck employee-customer-profit chain.

[15] Personal communication, Dr. Robert Kaplan, February 2000.

[16] For more on the Sears *Total Performance Indicators*, see Chapter 6.

[17] Edvinsson L., Malone M.S., *Intellectual Capital*. HarperBusiness Inc., New York, 1997.

[18] The Skandia Navigator divides metrics into perspectives similar to the Balanced Scorecard. Key areas of focus are: financial, customer, human, process, and renewal & development. Source: www.Skandia.com .

[19] *Globe and Mail*, Tuesday June 27, 2000.

[20] There are many valid concerns about patient confidentiality which still need to be addressed. For example, patients might be denied health insurance if insurers are made aware of their genetic predisposition to expensive diseases. The spectacular benefits of the Human Genome Project do not absolve us from ethical responsibility. We need to also ensure that use of genotype information is ethically sound.

[21] Carr, G. The Alchemists: The Pharmaceutical Industry Survey. Beyond the Behemoths, *The Economist*, February 21, 1998.

[22] Crosby P., *Quality is Free*, Penguin Books, Toronto, 1980. One of my favorite classics on quality.

Further Reading: Putting More Health Myths to Rest

[23] Personal communication, Dr. Jim Stewart, 1996. In his research on the world's safest companies, Dr. Stewart, Executive-in-Residence at the University of Toronto's Faculty of Management has developed data on the lost work injury frequency (LWIF) for a range of Canadian and international companies. He has found that some companies are up to several hundred times safer than the average, and up to a *thousand times* safer than the poor performers! Dupont Canada, for example had an average LWIF of .01 per 200,000 exposure hours, for the five years 1991—1995. This represents two lost work injuries in a work population of around 4,000. The Ontario manufacturing average for that period was around 5 LWIF, and for some large companies above 10. This represents a 500 and 1,000-fold difference. Shell Canada as a company for the same period had a LWIF of 0.17. While this was ten times worse than the experience of Dupont, it still represents very few lost-work injuries for a large company, and is still 25x better than the industry average.

[24] Personal communication, Dr. J.M. Stewart, 1999; and Stewart J.M., *Managing for World-Class Safety. Report on Research on the Management of Safety.* The Rotman School of Management, University of Toronto, June, 1999.

[25] Stewart J.M., *Op. cit.*

[26] Collins J.. C., Porras J.I. *Built to Last. Successful Habits of Visionary Companies.* HarperBusiness Inc., New York, 1994.

[27] Ted Pattenden, Speech to Occupational Health and Safety Conference, 1994. Industrial Accident Prevention Association, Toronto.

[28] It should be noted that National Rubber is not content with having an injury rate a mere fraction of their industry average, and is pushing for even better results.

[29] Personal communication, Dr. J.M. Stewart, 1998.

[30] Personal communication, Mark Henderson, Executive Vice President, The Clemmer Group, December 2000. www.clemmer.net .

[31] Personal communication, Martin Law, Team Leader, Employee and Family Assistance Program, and Member, Strategic Management Team and Multidisciplinary Wellness Strategy Team, City of Calgary, November, 2000. For more information on the City of Calgary, visit www.gov.calgary.ab.ca .

[32] For the definitive work on Strategy Maps, refer to Kaplan R.S., Norton D.P. Having trouble with your strategy? Then map it! *Op. cit.*

[33] *Ibid.*

[34] Block, Peter *The Empowered Manager: Positive Political Skills at Work.* Jossey-Bass, New York, 1991.

Chapter 2 (cont'd): Redefining Health and the Balanced Scorecard

[35] Personal communication, Dr. Martin Shain, October, 2000. Dr. Martin Shain is Head of the Workplace Program at Toronto's Centre for Addiction and Mental Health, and a leading light in Health Canada's workplace health research. He can be reached at mshain@arf.org .

[36] Personal communication, Lieutenant-Colonel David A. Wrather, Deputy Project Director, PMO – Quality of Life, National Defence Headquarters, May 2000.

[37] Lok, P. The Conference Board of Canada, *Smoking and the Bottom Line*, 1997.

[38] National Research Council Corporate Health Programs. *Clearing the Air: A Resource Guide for Smokers.* National Research Council, Ottawa, 1992.

[39] Malcolm Baldridge National Quality Program. *Criteria for Performance Excellence 2001, §5.3. Employee Well-being and Satisfaction.* United States Department of Commerce, National Institute of Standards and Technology. www.quality.nist.gov .

[40] Note that when I refer to "Stress" in this book, I'm referring to the kind of debilitating stress which erodes our performance and health—not the energizing kind of positive stress which can stimulate peak performance. For more on "Eustress", or this energizing stress, refer to the works of Hans Selye, pioneer of stress research.

[41] This 3.5% figure is derived from Fortune 100 statistics, correcting for the 18% of outliers who have more than 10 years of service. Source: Drake Beam Morin (DBM) United States, *CEO Tenure on Shaky Ground*, 1998.

[42] For more on the enduring merits of management systems, read Jim Collins' article Forget Strategy. Build Mechanisms Instead, reprinted from *Inc.*, October 1997, and available at www.jimcollins.com .

43 Collins J.C., Porras J.J. *Op. cit.*
44 *Ibid.*
45 BHAG: Big Hairy Audacious Goal. See Myth #6, Further Reading section.

CHAPTER 3:
TOP BOX RESULTS

46 Kirn, Steve. *Embedding HR Metrics in Total Performance Indicators*, presentation to HR Measurement Conference, International Quality and Productivity Center, Chicago, March, 2000.

47 For a comprehensive update on demographics, refer to David Foote's *Boom, Bust, and Echo 2000*, Stoddart Publishers, Toronto, 2000.

48 This is an unabashed oversimplification of the spectrum from satisfaction, to commitment, to loyalty... For more on this topic, refer to Reicheld F.F. *The Loyalty Effect; the hidden force behind growth, profits, and lasting value.* Harvard Business School Press, Boston, 1996; and Heskett J.L., Sasser W.E., Schlesinger L.A. *The Service-Profit Chain; how leading companies link profit and growth to loyalty, satisfaction, and value.* The Free Press, Toronto, 1997.

49 Kirn S., *Op. cit.*

50 Heskett J.L., *et al.*, *Op. cit.* See also Menezes M.A.J., Serbin J. *Xerox Corporation: The Customer Satisfaction Program.* Case 9-591-055. Harvard Business School Publishing, Boston, 1991.

51 O'Rourke F. *The Healthy Workplace: Celestica.* Presentation to The Bottom Line Conference: a conference marking World Mental Health Day in Canada. Calgary, October 20, 2000.

52 Personal communication, Neil McKendrick, Senior Transit Planner, Calgary Transit, City of Calgary, November 2000.

53 France built the Maginot Line after World War I to prevent future German invasions. It comprised a network of fortifications, underground bunkers, and forts.

54 Aggregate satisfied results represent all the positive results on a survey. For example, on a 6-point scale, if a 4 is "Slightly satisfied", 5 is "Satisfied", and 6 is "Very Satisfied", many organizations lump together their 4's, 5's and 6's into one aggregate score. While this looks good (results often indicate satisfaction in the 70—90% range), this is not nearly as

meaningful as differentiating the "Slightly" from the "Very" or "Totally" satisfied cadres.

[55] Kirn S., *Op. cit.*

[56] Source: The Gallup Organization. *The Gallup Path to Business Outcomes: Identify Strengths*, Gallup Website, November, 2000 (www.gallup.com/path/strengths/index.asp). Gallup is a Registered Trademark of The Gallup Organization

[57] MacLachlan R. Regeneration X. *People Management* 4:7. April 2, 1998. pp. 34-41.

[58] Happy ending? I am comforted that this particular organization, under new leadership, is now beginning to pursue "top box" results.

[59] As it turned out, the reason for this dramatic shift was dissatisfaction with traffic—a byproduct of a rapidly growing city. What is important in this example however, is how this substantial shift in top box satisfaction was concealed by the aggregate reporting of results.

[60] Maclachlan R., *Op. cit.*

[61] Personal communication, Neil McKendrick, Senior Transit Planner, City of Calgary, November, 2000.

[62] Kirn S. *Op. cit.*

[63] Reicheld F., Aspinwall K. Building High-Loyalty Business Systems, *Journal of Retail Banking*, Winter 1993 –1994.

[64] Bank One, *1999 Annual Report.*

[65] Kirn S. *Op. cit.*

[66] The introduction to the Reports on the Government Performance and Results Act from the United States General Accounting Office notes: "*The Government Performance and Results Act of 1993 seeks to shift the focus of government decision-making and accountability away from a preoccupation with the activities that are undertaken—such as grants dispensed or inspections made—to a focus on the results of those activities, such as real gains in employability, safety, responsiveness, or program quality.*" (www.gao.gov) For a sampling of other public sector Balanced Scorecard websites, see www.bscol.com, www.npr.gov, www.iqpc.com, www.va.gov/fedsbest, and www.gpra-institute.org .

[67] Photo source: Fergusson I.K. Shark Trust and Shark Specialist Group. From www.zoo.co.uk .

[68] Buckingham M., Coffman C. *First, Break all the Rules: What the World's Greatest Managers do Differently*. Simon & Schuster, New York, 1999.

[69] Icarus – the mythical Greek figure who escaped from prison with wings

made by his father, Daedalus. Icarus disregarded his father's warnings, flew too close to the sun, and perished when the glue on his wings melted.

70 Collins J. Perspectives Don't Rewrite the Rules of the Road, *Business Week*, August 28, 2000.

71 W.E. Deming, quality guru emphasized the importance of fostering pride of workmanship among employees. Deming rightly believed that this emotional response played a vital role in quality improvement.

72 Deming W.E., 14 Points for Management. *Out of the Crisis*. W. Edwards Deming Institute, Potomac, MD, 1986.

73 Belloc H., *The Silence of the Sea and other Essays*. Sheed and Ward. New York, 1940.

74 Gary Ross, Director. *Pleasantville*. Larger Than Life Productions. U.S.A., 1998.

75 Harry Rosen, as cited in the cover feature on stress: *MacLean's Magazine*, January 1996, 109:2, p32.

76 Semler R. *Maverick: The success story behind the world's most unusual workplace*. Tableturn Inc. Pub., New York, 1993.

77 F.F. Reicheld. *Op. cit.*

78 Heskett J.L., Sasser W.E., Schlesinger L.A. *Op. cit*. Reprinted with permission from the authors.

79 Tom Stephens was frequently cited in the media on safety. One example is from the *Globe and Mail*, January 1, 1997, in their Report on Business cover page.

80 As it turned out, when Tom Stephens left, MacMillan Bloedel was taken over by Weyerhaeuser Inc., which also has a strong focus on safety. So the house of cards did not collapse, and these safety results have in fact been improved upon. As Weyerhaeuser CEO Bill Gaynor noted at the November, 2000 conference in Vancouver, B.C. on The Business of Disability Management in the Forest Industry, *"There is nothing more important to us than safety. Our goal is to achieve a recordable incident rate of less than one (per 100 person years) in all our operations around the world."*

81 Personal communication, Tom Carson, Deputy Minister of Health, Manitoba, Canada, November, 2000. Tom Carson is now Deputy Minister, Culture, Heritage, and Tourism, but remains a leading light in health visioning in Canada.

82 Drake Beam Morin, *Op. cit.*

Chapter 4:
Good Health is Good Leadership

[83] For more information on the Health Project and National Health Awards, visit http://healthproject.stanford.edu .

[84] Getting Health Care's Priorities Straight, *Globe and Mail*, August 14, 2000.

[85] Dr. Peter Barrett in his Presidential Speech to the 133rd Annual General Meeting of the Canadian Medical Association. August 16, 2000.

[86] Sheremata D. Hail-busters. Battling Mother Nature in Alberta's Hail Valley. *Canadian Geographic*. July/August, 1998. p. 66.

[87] Sue Hills, visionary organizational health pioneer and Founder of the Alliance for Health and Fitness, Canada.

[88] Heskett J.L. *et al., Op cit.*

[89] Northwestern National Life Co. *Employee Burnout: Causes and Cures. Parts 1/2.* 1992.

[90] Kohler S., Kamp J. *American Workers Under Pressure Technical Report.* St. Paul Fire and Marine Insurance Company. St. Paul, 1992.

[91] Some additional reading on the topic of fairness, organizational justice, and dispute resolution includes FedEx's *Guaranteed Fair Treatment Procedure*, described in the American Management Association's *Blueprints for Service Quality: The Federal Express Approach*, 3rd Ed., New York, 1997; also Bowen D.E., Gilliland S.W., and Folger R.'s article on, "How being fair with employees spills over to customers", from *Organizational Dynamics*, 27:3, Winter, 1999; and Robert Folger's book, *Organizational Justice and Human Resources Management*, by Sage Publications, 1998.

[92] Lewin D., Schechter S., Four Factors Lower Disability Rates. *Personnel Journal*, November 1995 Supplement New Product, 74:11, p. 14.

[93] NORA Organization of Work document sourced from www.cdc.gov/niosh/nrworg.html

[94] Becker B.R., Huselid M.A., *The HR Scorecard: Linking People, Strategy, & Performance*. Balanced Scorecard Collaborative NetConference. September 14, 2000, p. 18.

[95] Cited from the Centres for Disease Control website: http://www.cdc.gov/niosh/ergtxt7.html#summary .

[96] In fact, Canada's Institute for Work and health reported a five-fold difference in Worker's Compensation health claims among five different

firms in the auto industry – a difference that is primarily attributed to how work at these firms is organized and performed. From Sullivan, T. *How Work Affects Health.* Presentation to the Institute for Health and Productivity Management, Toronto, October 2000.

[97] Cited from the Centres for Disease Control website: Stress at Work, http://www.cdc.gov/niosh/stresrel.html.

[98] Sauter SL, Murphy LR, Hurrell JJ, Jr. Prevention of work-related psychological disorders. *American Psychologist.* 1990, 45:10, pp.1146-1158.

[99] *Key Whitehall publications*: Marmot, M.G. Social differentials in health within and between populations. *Health and Wealth. Daedalus.* Vol. 123, 1994, pp. 197-215; and Marmot MG, Smith GD, Stansfeld S, Patel C, North F, Head J, White I, Brunner E, Feeney A. Health inequalities among British civil servants: the Whitehall II study. *Lancet* 1991;337:1387-1393; and Marmot M, Bosma H, Hemingway H, Brunner E, Stansfeld S. Contributions of job control and other risk factors to social variations in coronary heart disease incidence. *Lancet,* 1997. Vol. 350 pp. 235-239. For more information on the Whitehall Studies, visit http://www.workhealth.ort/projects/pwhitepub.htm.

[100] Marmot M., Bosma H., Hemingway H., Brunner E., Stansfield S. 1997, *Op. Cit.*

[101] Deming W.E., 14 Points for Management. *Out of the Crisis.* W. Edwards Deming Institute, Potomac, MD, 1986.

[102] Collins J. *And the Walls came Tumbling Down.* Copyright 1999. www.jimcollins.com. In this article, Jim comments on the permeability of structure in his own work environment: "*The whole key to the high performance climate on our research team is our use of mechanisms of commitment and connection rooted in freedom of choice.*"

[103] Personal communication, Dr. Martin Shain, October, 2000.

[104] Karasek R., Theorell T. *Op. cit.*

[105] Smith C. Sleep states and learning: A review of the animal literature. *Neuroscience and Biobehavioral Review.* 9, 1985. pp. 157 – 168.

[106] Shain M., Suurvali H. *Investing in Comprehensive Workplace Health Promotion.* Health Canada, December 2000.

[107] *Ibid.*

[108] Author's note: My apologies to the reader: I recall reading this reference, but have not been able to locate it to give due credit.

[109] For more on the effort/reward imbalance model, refer to Siegrist, J. Adverse health effects of high effort/low reward conditions. *Journal of Occupational Health Psychology* 1996; pp.27-41.

[110] Kaplan R.S., *The Balanced Scorecard*. Presentation to Balanced Scorecard for Government 2000 Conference, *Op. cit.*

[111] Corneil W., Barling J. *Work Habits, Working Conditions, and the Health of the Executive Cadre in the Public Service of Canada: A Synopsis of APEX's 1997 Study*. Association of Professional Executives of the Public Service of Canada, 1997. This report is available from the APEX website at www.apex.gc.ca.

[112] *Ibid.*

[113] *Ibid.*

[114] Personal communication, Dr. Martin Shain, 1998.

[115] Fergusson S., *MDS Nordion: Our Healthy Workplace*. Presentation to Conference Board of Canada, Council on Workforce Solutions, May 6, 2000.

[116] Smith G. *Work Rage: Identify the Problem, Implement the Solutions*. Harper Collins, Toronto, 2000.

[117] Personal communication, Gerry Smith, May 2000. Gerry Smith is Director of Specialty Services, Warren Shepell Consultants and author of the book *Work Rage*. For more information visit www.warrenshepell.com.

[118] McClay, CJ. Achieving breakthroughs in safety via employee empowerment. *Professional Safety* 40:12, December 1995 p.44-47.

[119] Worker's Compensation Board – Alberta, *1999 Annual Report*; and personal communication, Rob Crooks, Practice Leader, Health & Wellness, WCB—Alberta, November 2000.

[120] Sukay L.D. Safety programs alone don't work in reducing Worker's Compensation costs. *Risk Management*. September, 1993, pp. 43-49.

[121] National Rubber's name has since been changed to NRI Industries Inc.

[122] Ted Pattenden, Speech to OSH Conference 1994, *Op. cit.*

[123] Personal communication, Dr. Jim Stewart, 1998. NRI Industries is a privately held company, and does not release its specific profit figures.

[124] Shannon H.S., Overview of the Relationship between Organizational and Workplace Factors and Injury Rates. *Safety Science*, 26:3, 1997, pp. 201-217.

[125] Now we have specifics. For example, a poor social environment, characterized by high levels of negative conflict poses a greater risk to employees developing back pain, than do objective physical measures such as peak shear, and disk compression. Kerr M.S. 1997 PhD dissertation, as reported by Dr. Terry Sullivan, in his presentation *How Work affects Health*, to the Institute for Health and Productivity Management, Toronto, October 2000.

[126] Philbrick, Nathaniel *In the Heart of the Sea; The Tragedy of the Whaleship Essex*, Viking, Press, 2000.

[127] Conference Board of Canada. *Managing Corporate Health Care Costs*, 1995.

[128] Hoffman T., CIOs share retention tips. *Computerworld* 32:4, November 2, 1998, p. 16.

[129] Ganzel R., Putting out the welcome mat. *Training Magazine*. 35:3, March, 1998, pp. 54-62.

[130] Santa-Barbara, J., Shain M. When Workplace Stress Stifles Productivity. *Employee Health & Productivity Magazine*, January/February 1999, pp. 22-27. Dr. Jack Santa-Barbara is former CEO of Corporate Health Consultants, a leading Canadian Employee Assistance Provider, and one of Canada's *50 Best Managed Private Companies*. For more information visit the CHC website at www.chc-workingwell.ca .

[131] Sullivan T.J., *Op. cit.*

[132] Schlesinger L.A., Zornitsky J. Job Satisfaction, Service Capability, and Customer Satisfaction: An Examination of the Linkages and Management Implications. *Human Resource Planning*, 14:2, pp. 141 – 149.

[133] Ulrich D., Zenger J., Smallwood N. *Results-Based Leadership*. Harvard Business School Press, Boston, 1999.

[134] Becker B.R., Huselid M.A., Ulrich D. *The HR Scorecard: Linking People, Strategy, and Performance*. Harvard Business Publishing, Boston, 2001. (in press)

[135] Becker B.R., Huselid M.A., Balanced Scorecard Collaborative NetConference, September 14, 2000. *The HR Scorecard: Linking People, Strategy, & Performance*.

[136] Adapted to highlight key capability/health drivers from Dr. Huselid and Becker's slides, Balanced Scorecard Collaborative NetConference, September 14, 2000. Reprinted with permission from the authors.

[137] See Ulrich's works: Organizational Capability: Competing from the Inside/Out" (with Dale Lake). *Academy of Management Executive* 5:1, 1991. pp. 77-91, or Profiling Organizational Competitiveness: Cultivating Capabilities." *Human Resource Planning* 16:3, 1993. pp. 1-17. For more of Dr. Ulrich's publications, see http://www.bus.umich.edu/academic/faculty/dou.html .

[138] Ulrich D., Zenger J., Smallwood J. *Results-Based Leadership*. Harvard Business School Press, Boston, 1999.

[139] Buckingham M., Coffman C. *First, Break all the Rules: What the World's Greatest Managers do Differently*. Simon & Schuster, New York, 1999.

[140] *Ibid.*
[141] *Canada @ Work™. The Corporate Rewards of Flexibility and Balance.* © Royal Bank of Canada, 1999.
[142] The Best & Worst Jobs. *MacLean's* Business Cover Story. May 31, 1999.
[143] Prudential Insurance Study on Recruitment and Retention success, as cited by Dr. Lenora Peters Gant in *Strategic Planning Linked to Bottom Line Expectations*, at HR Measurement, International Quality and Productivity Centre, Chicago, March 2000.
[144] Betcherman G., McMullen K., Leckie N., Caron C., *The Canadian Workplace in Transition; Final Report of the Human Resource Management Project.* Industrial Relations Centre, Queens University at Kingston, 1994.
[145] *Ibid.*
[146] Collins J. Built to Flip, *Fast Company*, March 2000.
[147] Personal Communication: Dr. Martin Shain, August 2000.
[148] These questions are based on key components of capability, as defined by Schlesinger and Zornitsky, *Human Resources Planning*, 14:9, *Op. cit.* For a more rigorous examination of the Cycle of Capability, refer to Figure 7-4, *Questions associated with the Cycle of Capability*, from Heskett et al., *The Service Profit Chain.*

Chapter 5: If Quality can be Free, Health can be Too!

[149] The PIMS database can be referenced at the Strategic Planning Institute, www.thespinet.org .
[150] For a classic book on Service/Quality excellence, refer to Jim Clemmer's *Firing on all Cylinders: The Service/Quality System for High-Powered Corporate Performance.* MacMillan Canada, 2nd Ed., Toronto, 1992.
[151] Deming W.E., *Minerva* News, March 1993, p.3.
[152] Downey A., Kudar R., The High Cost of Health. *CMA Magazine.* April, 1995. pp. 12 – 14.
[153] Examples of Costs: a) *Detection:* Customer loyalty, employee engagement audits. Health risk appraisals. b) *Prevention:* Investment in cultural transformation, ergonomic design, work/life optimization c) *Direct failure costs*: WCB premiums, drug costs, disability costs. d) *Indirect failure costs*: Replacement costs for absent workers, turnover costs; e)

Opportunity Costs: These represent income that is foregone because of poor wellbeing, and form the underbelly of the health cost iceberg! Examples of opportunity costs include lost productivity, quality, and creativity from stressed, ill, injured, or demoralized workers.

[154] Kuttner, Robert. Health Policy Report: The American Health Care System – Employer-Sponsored Health Coverage. *The New England Journal of Medicine.* January 21, 1999, 340:3.

[155] I'm making the assumption that detection of health problems represents a good cost, even if it is after the fact, since we can prevent the severity of health problems through effective health management. That said, it is always better to detect upstream indicators, rather than after-the-fact outcomes. For example, it is arguably better to detect stressors in the workplace through an employee audit, than to wait until these stressors materialize, and then to hold a blood-pressure clinic to pick up the casualties of stress.

[156] Calgary Asthma Program, *Information Brochure*, 2000.

[157] Personal communication, Lise Jantzon's, Manager, Customer Relations Alberta, Glaxo Wellcome Inc., December 2000.

[158] Troy T.N. Glaxo Wellcome Asthma Program breathes new life into self-management, *Managed Healthcare*, 8:9, September 1998.

[159] Cenicerous R. Self-wired health plan connects at Motorola. *Business Insurance*, 31:47, November 1997, pp. 1, 36.

[160] Government of Ontario Press Release: *Free Flu Shot for All Ontarians Beginning Today.* November 1, 2000. www.newswire.ca/government/ontario .

[161] Kaplan R.S. *The Balanced Scorecard.* Presentation to BSC for Government Conference. *Op. cit.*

[162] Becker B.R., Huselid M.A., *The HR Scorecard: Linking People, Strategy, & Performance.* Balanced Scorecard Collaborative NetConference, *Op. cit.*

[163] Personal communication, Ted Pattenden, November 28, 2000.

[164] Ted Pattenden, presentation to Industrial Accident Prevention Association Conference 2000, Toronto, Ontario. www.iapa.ca .

[165] Chisholm J., Bamji P. *The National Rubber Company* (Case Study B). Queen's University School of Business, 1996.

[166] Stewart J.M. The Multi-Ball Juggler. *Business Quarterly*, Summer, 1993.

[167] C. Everett Koop National Health Award Winners, 1996. *Description: Pitney Bowes Corporation*, from www.healthproject.stanford.edu/koop .

[168] Personal Communication, Dr. Jack Santa-Barbara, CEO CHC-Working Well, March, 1999.

[169] Applied Management Consultants. *The Annual Employer Survey: Trends and Issues in Private Drug Plans.* Toronto, 1998.

[170] Foss Krista, Diabetes Cured in Lab Rats, *The Globe and Mail*, November 23, 2000.

[171] Personal communication, Sean Sullivan, President and CEO, the Institute of Health and Productivity Management. For more information on the Institute of Health and Productivity Management, visit www.ihpm.org .

[172] Personal communication, Peter Simpson, Glaxo Smith Kline, January 2001.

[173] See Chapter 6 for a summary of *Health Evidence*™, the vehicle we use to identify key health issues.

[174] Personal communication, Lise Jantzon, Manager, Customer Relations, Alberta, Glaxo Wellcome, November, 2000.

[175] Robinson K.S. New Study Shows Most Prevalent and Expensive Workforce Illnesses. Strategic Human Resources Management, *Society for Human Resource Management (SHRM) Online*, September 26, 2000. Findings from this study: *the 5 most expensive physical conditions were:* coronary heart, gastrointestinal disorders, hypertension, vaginal delivery, and osteoarthritis. *The 5 most expensive mental health conditions were:* bipolar disorder (major depressive episode), neurotic, personality and nonpsychotic disorders; depression; alcoholism; and anxiety disorder.

[176] Kuttner, Robert. Health Policy report, The American Health Care System, Employer-Sponsored Health Coverage, *New England Journal of Medicine*, 340:3, January 21, 1999.

[177] Personal communication, Wolfgang Zimmermann, National Institute for Disability Management and Research, November 2000; and Scheer, Steven (Ed.), *Assessing the Vocational Capacity of the Impaired Worker.* Aspen Publishers, 1990.

Chapter 6: Linking Health into the Balanced Scorecard

[178] Rucci A.J. et al., *Op. cit.* The Conference Board of Canada wrote a similar report on the Canadian experience in Brooks E.R., *Loyal Customers, Enthusiastic Employees, and Corporate Performance*. Conference Board of Canada, Report # 231-98.

[179] Then again, maybe IBM and its spin-offs will have the last laugh as mainframes come back into vogue.

[180] For more background on the Organization of Work, take a look at the National Institute of Safety and Health's website information on the "Organization of Work": http://www.cdc.gov/niosh/nrworg.html .

[181] Key components of a healthy workplace are presented, as summarized from Chapter 4.

[182] Sears index measures are derived from Rucci *et al.*, *Op. cit.*

[183] Buckingham M., Coffman C. *Op. cit.*

[184] The Gallup Path is Copyright© 1997 The Gallup Organization. Reprinted with permission The Gallup Organization. Source: http://www.gallup.com/path/index.asp .

[185] Kaplan R.S. *The Balanced Scorecard*. Presentation to Balanced Scorecard for *Government 2000 Conference*, *Op. cit.*

[186] Hoheisel W., Wheeler E. *The Department of Transportation's use of the Procurement Balanced Scorecard*. Presentation to Balanced Scorecard for Government Conference, International Quality & Productivity Centre, Washington D.C., January, 2000.

[187] Malcolm Baldridge National Quality Program. *Criteria for Performance Excellence 2001, §5.3. Employee Well-being and Satisfaction*. United States Department of Commerce, National Institute of Standards and Technology. www.quality.nist.gov .

[188] Maslow, A. A theory of human motivation. *Psychological Review*, 50, 1943. pp. 370-396.

[189] Heskett *et. al.*, *Op. cit.*

[190] Loeppke R. *Journal of Occupational & Environmental Medicine*. March, 1997.

[191] Personal communication, Dr. Lynda Robson, Institute for Work and Health, December 2000. Canada's Institute for Work and Health is working on a "*Healthy Workplace*" Balanced Scorecard which diagrams the causal linkages for determinants of health between four scorecard

categories: 1) Implementation of Healthy Workplace initiatives; 2) Workplace Determinants of Job exposures 3) Hazardous Job exposures; and 4) Health outcomes. For more on the *Healthy Workplace* Balanced Scorecard, visit www.iwh.on.ca .

[192] Kaplan R., Norton D., Having Trouble with your Strategy? Then Map it. *Op. cit.;* and Kaplan R.S., Norton D.P. *The Strategy-Focused Organization. Op. cit.*

[193] With author's apologies – this is an archive I have not been able to reference.

[194] General Election 1997 News: *Blair's Bureaucracy Buster to Rescue Red Tape NHS,* sourced from www.ge97.com .

[195] Rucci A.J., *Op. cit.*

[196] Buckingham M., Coffman C. *Op. cit.*

[197] Abraham Maslow, *Motivation and Personality,* Harper Publishing, New York, 1954.

[198] *Verboten* – German for "forbidden".

[199] American Management Association. *Blueprints for Service Quality; The Federal Express Approach.* AMA Membership Publications Div., New York, 1997.

[200] This sampling of FedEx's Service Quality Indicators is excerpted from, American Management Association Management Briefing, *Op. cit.*

[201] Hoheisel W., Wheeler E. *Op. cit.*

[202] Personal communication, Mark Henderson, Executive Vice President, The Clemmer Group, December 2000.

[203] The Business Health Culture Index, copyright Health Canada, 2000. Cited with permission from Health Canada.

[204] Adapted from Shain M., *Stress, Satisfaction, and Health at Work.* (Published in *OHS Canada* as Stress and Satisfaction, April/May 1999, pp. 38 – 47; and Shain M., Suurvali H. *Op. cit.* Reprinted and adapted with permission from Health Canada.

[205] The Multiple Health Risk Score. Cited with permission from Health Canada.

[206] Personal communication, Martin Law, Team Leader for the City of Calgary's Employee and Family Assistance Program, and member of the City's Multidisciplinary Wellness Strategy Team and Strategic Management Team, City of Calgary, November 2000.

[207] Kohler S., Kamp J. *Op. cit.*

[208] Coren S., *Sleep Thieves.* Free Press, Toronto, 1996.

[209] See Chapter 5 for the discussion of Cost of Health accounting.
[210] Karasek R., Theorell T., *Healthy Work*, Basic Books, 1990.
[211] The male profile is similar to the female profile presented. Refer to Karasek R., Theorell, *Op. cit*, Figures 2-4a and 2-4d.
[212] I am making a significant, albeit credible leap here from stress to depression. For more research on how sustained workplace stress translates into depression, I recommend the works of W. (Bill) Wilkerson, President of the Business and Economic Roundtable on Mental Health. Mr. Wilkerson can be reached at the Business Roundtable residence at GPC Communications in Toronto, Canada, Tel: 416 598-0055 Ext. 271.
[213] Office of the Governor. *State agencies tear up 2,000 pages of rules, Governor Locke announces*. Press Release, December 1, 2000, from State of Washington's website: www.access.wa.gov .
[214] Note: This drug information is only made available to the corporation and researchers in aggregate form, with all identifying information for patients removed, other than their business unit—as long as their business unit has more than 1,000 employees. In this way, no attribution can be made with any individual's prescription profile, yet we are able to compare differences across business units.
[215] Prescription patterns from IMS Health, Canada reflect estimated occurrences, by claim. This data is sourced from IMS' *Sub-Disease Occurrence Predictions*, November 30, 2000.
[216] By rights, "Repetitive Strain Injuries" (RSI's) such as carpal tunnel syndrome should fall under "Musculoskeletal Injuries"(MSK). But due to the prevalence of RSI's, and the continuing high impact of other MSK injuries, these have been divided into two groups. Note there is some variation between this list, and that derived from Health Evidence. For the first Index, the Wellness Team chose to address musculoskeletal injuries and repetitive strain injuries separately, and therefore we are not yet addressing digestive disorders noted earlier in Chapter 5.
[217] Community Asthma Care Centres. *Program Evaluation: The Impact of Patient Assessment and Education on Asthma Health Status*. A Glaxo Wellcome Partnership Approach in Asthma Management. Mississauga, December 2000. Reproduced with permission from Glaxo Wellcome.
[218] *Ibid*.
[219] Kaplan R.S., Norton D.P. *The Strategy-Focused Organization. Ibid*.
[220] Phillips J.J., Stone R.D., Phillips P.P. *The Human Resources Scorecard: Measuring the Return on Investment*. Jack J. Phillips is Chairman and CEO of the Jack Phillips Center for Research, a division of FranklinCovey.

[221] Becker B.R., Huselid M.A., Ulrich D., *Op. cit.*

[222] Verizon's HR Scorecard was spearheaded by Randall MacDonald, EVP of HR for GTE, and Garrett Walker, scorecard project leader, under the GTE umbrella. Verizon Communications Inc. was formed from the merger of GTE and Bell Atlantic.

[223] Zagarow, Herb. *Using the Balanced Scorecard to Link Performance Measures and Strategic Plans to your Agency's Budget Process*. Balanced Scorecard for Government 2000 Conference, International Quality and Productivity Centre, Washington, 2000.

[224] Rene Ewing, State of Washington, *Evolution of Performance Management Using the Balanced Scorecard*. Presentation to BSC for Government 2000 Conference, Washington D.C., 2000.

[225] For a color version of this figure, visit www.HealthyScorecard.com .

[226] The concept of an Overtime Risk Index is particularly timely for the transportation industry, where grueling schedules and sleep deprivation take their toll through highway tragedy. While some overtime is favored by drivers and managers, there is clearly an objective threshold where this becomes a substantial safety risk. It is this threshold that we want to capture in the Overtime Risk Index.

[227] Personal communication, Martin Lesperance 2000. Martin Lesperance can be reached through www.safete.com .

[228] Martin Lesperance's newsletter, www.FamilySafe.com .

[229] Labovitz G., Rosansky V. *The Power of Alignment: How great companies stay centered and accomplish extraordinary things*. John Wiley & Sons, New York, 1997. This book packs a punch. I particularly enjoy the authors' description of and/and leadership: "*Alignment gives managers at every level of the organization the ability to: Rapidly deploy a coherent business strategy; be totally customer focused; develop world-class people; continuously improve business processes—all at the same time.*"

[230] Demetriou B., *FedEx's Survey Feedback Action Process*. Presentation to HR Measurement 2000 Conference, International Quality and Productivity Centre, Chicago, 2000.

[231] Personal communication, Bill Wilkerson, President, National Business and Economic Roundtable on Mental Health, 1999.

[232] Gottfried Grafström. *Words of Value: A conversation with Leif Edvinsson*, Skandia, and Arne Richtnér, Ericsson Business Consulting. Skandia, 1999; and *Human Capital in Transformation. Intellectual Capital Prototype Report*. Skandia, 1998.

[233] The *HR Action Centre*, as presented by Hewitt & Associates in *HR*

Measurement at American Express: A successful journey and a new road ahead, at HR Measurement Conference 2000, International Quality & Productivity Centre, Chicago, 2000.

[234] The Sears Roebuck *Success Sharing* intranet, as presented by Dr. Steve Kirn, VP Innovation and Organization Development, *Embedding HR Metrics in Total Performance Indicators,* HR Measurement Conference, International Quality and Productivity Center, San Francisco, 2001.

[235] Kaplan R.S. *The Balanced Scorecard.* Presentation to Balanced Scorecard for Government Conference 2000. *Op. cit.*

[236] For more information on the Institute for Work and Health and the Healthy Workplace Scorecard, contact Dr. Lynda Robson or Dr. Terrence Sullivan at www.iwh.on.ca .

[237] Becker B.R., Huselid M.A., *The HR Scorecard: Linking People, Strategy, & Performance.* Balanced Scorecard Collaborative NetConference, *Op. cit.*

[238] The Jack Phillips Center for Research can be reached through www.roipro.com .

[239] The Saratoga Institute can be reached through www.saratogainstitute.com .

[240] For more information on the International Quality & Productivity Centre's outstanding conferences on the Balanced Scorecard and HR Measurement, visit www.iqpc.com .

[241] For Skandia's recent advances in Intellectual Capital management, visit www.skandia.com .

[242] Terminology is based on Federal Express' *Survey Feedback Action* process, as outlined in American Management Association, *Op. cit.*

[243] For more on Strategy Maps, refer to Kaplan R.S., Norton D.P., Having Trouble with your Strategy? Then Map it. *Op. cit.,* or Kaplan R.S., Norton D.P. *The Strategy-Focused Organization, Op. cit.*

Chapter 7:
The Big Picture

[244] Buckingham M., Coffman C. *Op. cit.*

[245] Loeppke R. U.S. health costs exceed one trillion dollars. *Op. cit.*

[246] Jim Collins, Shareflipping Cheats Shareholders of Real Value. *USA Today*, Feb 24, 2000.

[247] The PIMS database can be referenced at the Strategic Planning Institute, www.thespinet.org .

[248] The "accountability gorillas" – gratefully cited from Epstein M.J., Birchard B., in *Counting what Counts: Turning Corporate Accountability to Competitive Advantage.* Perseus Books, Reading, 1999.

[249] Becker B.R., Huselid M.A. *The HR Scorecard: Linking People, Strategy, & Performance.* Balanced Scorecard Collaborative NetConference, *Op. cit.*

[250] *Ibid.*

[251] Ernst & Young LLP. *Measures that Matter™.* 1997.

[252] Watson Wyatt. *The Human Capital Index: Linking Human Capital and Shareholder Value.* Information on this index is available at www.watsonwyatt.com .

[253] Other forays in the Human Capital/Value equation include: Hewitt's report, *Are the 100 Best Better?: An Empirical Investigation of the Relationship between being a Best Employer and Firm Performance.* March, 2,000; *The Dow Jones Sustainability Group Index* ranks leaders in organizational sustainability, according to how well they manage sustainability opportunities and risks. These are grouped into five categories: innovation, governance (including corporate culture), shareholders, leadership, and society. For more on the Dow Jones Sustainability Group Index, visit www.sustainability-index.com .

[254] Bank of Montreal. News Release: *Bank of Montreal Executive Named Vice-Chair of Canadian Business and Economic Round Table on Mental Health.* www.newswire.ca/releases/January/1999; and personal communication, Maria Gonzales, Vice President, Strategic Initiatives, Bank of Montreal, October 2000. Maria Gonzales is a highly respected leader in organizational health, and has been deeply involved in the bank's *Shifting the Performance Curve* initiative. This thrust focuses on three pillars: "*attracting and retaining top talent, creating the conditions to foster and sustain a highly effective workplace with above-average performance, and inspiring a high level of employee commitment*" (Bank of

Montreal, *1999 Annual Report*).

[255] Peters T., quotation cited by Grafström G., Edvinsson L. *Accounting for Minds: An Inspirational Guide to Intellectual Capital.* Skandia 1998.

[256] Ignatieff N. A New Force in Injury Prevention. *Accident Prevention.* July/August, 1996; and personal communication, Patricia Coursey, President, Safe Communities Foundation, December 2000. The Safe Communities Foundation can be contacted through www.safecommunities.ca .

[257] Duerr A. *Living the Ethical City.* 2000 State of the City Address, Rotary Club of Calgary, Tuesday January 18, 2000.

[258] Section 9 of the *Canada Health Act* describes the principle of Comprehensiveness: "...*the health care insurance plan of a province must insure all insured health services provided by hospitals, medical practitioners or dentists...*"

[259] Bell Canada Media Relations. *News Release: Government of Alberta awards $300 million network investment to Bell.* Calgary, Alberta. November 2, 2000.

[260] Personal communication, Sean Sullivan, President and CEO, Institute for Health and Productivity Management, December 2000. For more information on the Institute for Health and Productivity Management, visit www.ihpm.org .

[261] *Vision Statement 2000:* Worker's Compensation Board – Alberta, available from www.wcb.ab.ca .

[262] Stop Thief! Assessing the Impact of Migraine in the Workplace. *Special Report of Employee Health & Productivity Magazine*, Fall, 1997. pp. 11-13.

[263] Migraine in the Workplace. *Special Report, Employee Health & Productivity Magazine.* 5:6, Fall, 1997.

[264] Kaplan R.S., *The Balanced Scorecard*, Presentation to Balanced Scorecard for Government conference 2000. *Op. cit.*

[265] Personal communication, Dr. Robert S. Kaplan, December 2000.

[266] Personal communication, Mark Henderson, Executive Vice President, The Clemmer Group. December, 2000.

[267] Personal communication, Owen Griffiths, Senior Consultant, Tecskor Software Inc., www.tecskor.com .

"... to leave the world a little better;

whether by a healthy child, a garden patch

or a redeemed social condition;

to know even one life has breathed easier

because you have lived.

This is the meaning of success."

Ralph Waldo Emerson

The Healthy Scorecard is available at special discounts for bulk purchases. For more information contact Healthy Business Inc. at:

Healthy Business Inc., 43 Sunwood Way S.E.,
Calgary, Alberta, T2X 2W5, CANADA
Fax: (403) 201-4052, or visit www.HealthyScorecard.com

For more information on the Healthy Scorecard, visit www.HealthyScorecard.com

ISBN 1-55212-557-2